The Dream Codes Lectures

The Dream Codes Lectures

Anna Aragno

IPBOOKS.net
International Psychoanalytic Books

International Psychoanalytic Books (IPBooks)
New York • http://www.IPBooks.net

Published by IPBooks, Queens, NY
Online at: www.IPBooks.net

On the Cover: "Freud for Anna" H. Cardo, by kind permission of the
Horacio Cardo estate.

ISBN: 978-1-969031-00-7

*To all my loves, great and small, transient, lasting and everlasting,
each and all have taught me to try to understand more.*

In the collapse of everything valuable, the psychology alone has remained untouched. The dream [book] stands entirely secure and my beginnings of metapsychological work have only grown in my estimation.

—*Sigmund Freud, Letter to Fliess of September 21, 1897,*
Masson, 1985, p. 266.

But when it came to dreams, it was no longer dealing with a pathological symptom, but with a phenomenon of normal mental life ... If dreams turned out to be constructed like symptoms ... then psychoanalysis was no longer an auxiliary science in the field of psychopathology, it was rather the starting-point of a new and deeper science of the mind. ... Its postulates and findings could be carried over to other regions of mental happening; a path lay open ... that led far afield, into spheres of universal interest.

—*Sigmund Freud, 1925, p. 47.*

A sign is something which, offering itself to the senses, conveys something other than itself to the intellect.

—*Augustine, De Doctrina Christiana, 389 AD. II,1.*

Table of Contents

A Personal Introduction

The Interpretation of Dreams contains, even according to my present-day judgement, the most valuable of all discoveries it has been my good fortune to make. Insight such as this falls to one's lot but once in a lifetime.
—*S. Freud, Preface to 3rd Ed. 1931, p. xxxii*

From a very young age, I felt a resonant response to Freud's writings. Yet psychoanalysis was a second passion, a study into which I entered midstream in life after a career in one of the arts. After a degree in human development, I tailored my Master's to follow Freud's recommendation for future analysts, a palette of interdisciplinary subjects. Of theoretical bent, and given to high abstraction, I was drawn to metapsychology—Freud's core interest, unfortunately abandoned by the field; my doctoral thesis became an expanded revision of the Topographical model. After my dissertation proposing a revised developmental model of mind based on Symbolization (published by IUP, 1997) a door opened that led unexpectedly to a long writing career as a theoretical revisionist. In 2009, my paper on empathy, published in *JAPA,* received two academic commentaries: one by the neuroscientist V. Gallese, another by a professor of semiotics, Donald Favareau, the latter inviting me to Prague for a Biosemiotics conference. This introduction to an international world of cutting-edge academics integrating biology and semiotics, all reading similar interdisciplinary works, bent towards merging the sciences and humanities, and all *highly* animated in intellectual discussion, piqued my interest. Albeit feeling like a fish out of water, I was hooked! As the only psychoanalyst, I tailored my talks to both inform and integrate many specifically psychoanalytic phenomena and principles across a wide range of subjects, but always with the unique human capacity for symbolization as core concept, and Freud's "dream theory" as focal point of entry. This collection of lectures, emerging out of these international conferences held in many of the major historical universities across Europe, are the contents of this book.

A little background: By invitation, I started with the Biosemiotics community then moved to Code Biology, an offshoot group led by M. Barbieri, a theoretical biologist, Professor of embryology at the University of Ferrara, who began his career in Cambridge working with Crick on decoding the DNA double helix. Whereas both interdisciplinary groups engage in studying all signs in living systems, and their charters are similar, they differ in some crucial ways: The older Biosemiotics community adheres to a Piercean triadic definition of the "sign," even at organic cellular levels, implying "interpretive" capacities, of sorts, to molecules. The Code Biology model, rather, begins with binary codes, moving from molecular, to neural, to cultural coding processes, through three foundational macro-evolutionary stages each marked by different semiotic forms. This fundamental difference may at first appear merely definitional but its significance has deeper conceptual and theoretical implications, especially for the study of reference and how meanings are made. For this, and other reasons that will become clear, I followed Professor Barbieri and moved to the Code Biology group. Its broader code-based evolutionary and epigenetic conceptual framework fit well with work I had already done (Aragno 1997/2016, 2006/2016) in revising our general model of mind and communication, and offered greater amplitude of challenges in the current *Weltanschauung* of a slowly changing paradigm. After all, it was Freud's decoding of the signifying mechanisms of the Primary Process in dreams that led to the founding models and theories of psychoanalysis and all his writings on unconscious processes that ensued.

The conferences were spearheaded under the leadership and core ideas of Marcello Barbieri, progenitor of the integration of coding and semiosis into the biological sciences (Barbieri,1985, 2006a,b). The principal tenet of Barbieri's theory is that coding processes are at the center of major macroevolutionary shifts, the charter of his group, to promote international scholars and researchers to engage in the interdisciplinary study of *all* codes of life. This new semantic slant to the study of natural and cultural codes introduces modes of meaning-making in various forms and at various levels of organismic organization along evolutionary lines. His theoretical vision belongs in the wider *Zeitgeist* of a general *information* paradigm breaking from the hitherto sharply divided humanities and natural sciences. In a trend that began in the quantum revolution, gaining momentum in the fifties and sixties in different disciplines, from DNA to family therapy, systems theory to interpersonal dynamics, interest turned from "things" themselves to what happens *between* them. In philosophical spheres we became less interested in *what* we know than *how* we know it.

Viewing the organism as essentially active introduces the concept of innate development and wholeness in preserving the "disequilibrium of steady state" (von Bertalanfy, 1968, 209): *coherence* occurs spontaneously between interacting systems that come into constant contact. What has impact and what is impacted upon, invoking Heisenberg, will *always* have to be understood as a dialectic, in terms of recursivity. Principles of *form and transforming organizations* are the scientific "laws" for living systems; their analysis cannot be guided by quantified research or principles of hard determinism.

And this is precisely the point: the challenge in the vigorous inter-disciplinarity involved in studying multiple interactive processes and phenomena at different levels of systemic organization offered immense possibilities for amplifying my revision of our psychoanalytic general model of mind and communication while also posing some daunting problems of communication. Due to the sheer volume of knowledge accrued in each discipline, the high level of specialization creates isolates of scholarship, each living in its own cognitive frame of reference, using its own vocabulary of terms. A commonplace word may have a completely different meaning in engineering than in psychoanalysis. Yet coming together now requires that we speak *to each other,* and in ways that break-through the barriers of the portentous academic tower of Babel that looms over these gatherings! We use the same words in different ways; the molecular folks can't metaphorize the imagistic language of the human unconscious in which psychoanalysts live daily! I, for one, get dizzy just looking at digital computations; the computer scientists and mathematicians cannot move outside their equation-driven climate. And, most dramatic of all, those stuck in the "hard" versus "soft" science framework cannot make the leap from physical/organic chemo-code-guided rules to the psychological realm where *functional-form* and morphology spell organization in the multidetermined condensed domain of multiple meanings! Yet the communal interest in what happens in coded *inter-actions* between living systems at *all levels of organization* demands that we each bring what we know to the table as the group struggles along trying to decipher each other's semantic frame of reference.

Psychoanalysis operates on the assumption that unconscious motives and meanings are reflected in all that is said and done. Manifest behaviors and speech acts are not just clues to the workings of minds; they *are* those workings. This applies most specially to dreams, a true coded revelation of what is *in* and *on* our minds and what we think and feel about it. The mind's most complex defensive layered workings are displayed in these emotional sense-images spun into linguistic narratives that can be read much like an MRI by those competent to interpret them. It is difficult to overestimate the importance of dreams in psychoanalysis; they remain the centrepiece of our theory of mind; to us, what the telescope was to Galileo.

Through this universal phenomenon of the deepest unconscious, we see the mind's basic manifest/latent *semiotic structuring* in the "dream-work," a semantic composed of signifying mechanisms in pictographic, metaphoric and metonymic, patterned meaning-forms. In the formal regression to the "primary process," Freud saw a telescoping back in time, potentially to our species' earlier modes of cognition, anticipating that "psycho-analysis may claim a high place among the sciences which are concerned with the reconstruction of the earliest and most obscure periods of the beginning of the human race" (Freud, 1900, p. 549). But few in our field have ventured further than where Freud left off. Today, with the help of an organismic biosemiotic developmental model of mind supplemented by extensive cross-referencing from paleo-anthropology, neuroscience, early development, semiotic and Code Biology principles, while still adhering to a basic premise of psychoanalytic methodology that the *manifest expresses latent meanings in understanding mind,* there are more evolutionary signs from our prehistory to be uncovered and understood.

The scientific analysis of dreams was the birth of psychoanalysis yielding its first theory of mind. Although Freud pointed to the "as if," "just like," innuendos in dream formation, uncovering its four meaning-making primary-process mechanisms, today we recognize that the dream is also *metaphorically* structured, pointing to *this* to mean *that*. Compelled by the scientific *Weltanschauung* of his day to look for causes, Freud had instead stumbled on *meanings*. Embedded in a medical community that demanded physicalist explanations, his focus on the motivating "wish" detracted from the more formidable unveiling of the underpinnings of human signifying processes. *Understanding* rather than *explanation* would become

4

the philosophical stance for psychoanalysis. Without the deterministic requirement, the "motive force" for dreams need not be couched in terms of "wish-fulfilment" but in the functional forms of *cognizing* itself: in attempts at *re*-presenting, a first picturing in order to figure things out; in giving expression to a repressed affect, shaping a subjective state, encapsulating adaptive strategies to metabolize, organize, and make sense of experience. In this light, the dream's *signifying* forms reveal another way of thinking, the motive force for this nocturnal phenomenon, its *own operative activities*. And because a "mode of thought" is not a force but a *function* of how the human nervous system and brain "work," we may infer a *formulative principle* issuing from deep organic layers of sensory-affective response.

For me the dream is the entry-point for unconscious processes as well as a bridge from soma to psyche and, through language, for making the unconscious conscious. Hence, the title of the series and its preeminently psychoanalytic foundations. The overriding goal behind all my writings is to fulfill Freud's vision, to advance our meta-theory and scientific method, to update and expand its findings and contribute to universal knowledge. But I am not a biologist. Having laid down a revised model of mind and communication, my goals in unifying the biological and psychological became severely challenged by Professor Barbieiri and, more gently, by T. Shapiro, stretching from microcellular coding to cerebral signifying inter-active processes at multiple levels of organization. In a nutshell; to peer *beneath* the dream at organic sensory processes along evolutionary lines. Curtailed in movement by the Covid pandemic lockdown (2020), I took the oportunity to arm myself with a host of new books, and tackled a vast new reading list in paleo-anthropology, neuro- and evolutionary-psychology, brain and cultural development, so that the last several talks present my intergration of this broad new range of interdisciplinary fields. My questions were: What occurs *before* the neural clustering of "dynamic schematization"? What came before the metaphoric structuring and primary-process signifying mechanisms of the dream-codes? How did the human brain/mind evolve to use this coagulant process to subjectively picture experienced stimuli?

I want to express my deep gratitude to Professors M. Barbieri (Ferrara University) and D. Favareau (National University of Singapore) for their steadfast encouragement, and for enabling me to participate regularly in these stimulating international academic gatherings. Behind them stand other great professor/mentors like J. Bruner and R. Sapolsky (the New School NYC), C. Brenner, T. Shapiro, and A. Richards (NY Psychoanalytic), E. Marcus (Columbia Group), and N. Freidman (IPTAR), without whose interest and encouragement I might not have ventured far. They all supported my challenging quest to dare to push the conceptual boundaries of our research methodology, as Freud wished, beyond the clinical domain. Most of all, though certainly a fish out of water, I thank them all for having made me feel less of one!

The book moves chronologically, beginning with the formation and establishment of the split-off organization and the first Code Biology Conference in Paris in 2014, to the present time. Threaded throughout, I strive to join body and mind, and finally to land on some evolutionary principle or template that may have led to the emergence of a uniquely human attribute—the capacity to *re-present* a mental image—our dominant semiotic advantage. Insofar as there is much that joins us to the animal kingdom, we diverge dramatically in this crucial endowment, singled out in evolution, enabling hominids to record, design, calculate, communicate, and, yes, *dream* and *imagine,* as only humans can.

A word about the prestigious venues like La Sorbonne, Paris; Jena University, Germany; Urbino University, Italy; the University of Granada, Spain; and Olomouc University, Czech Republic; some established in the fifteenth and sixteenth centuries, of extraordinary historical import and beauty, and especially the lively excursions, treks, hikes, museum-visits, and unforgettable dinner-locations, we all enjoyed so much. The title becomes self-explanatory in reading the lectures; the dream in psychoanalysis as portal to the deep unconscious. Throughout, the importance of Freud's decoding of this pictorial language weaves through the fabric of every lecture as does the echo of his deepest wish: that psychoanalytic research advance its meta-theorical premises, deepening our understanding of the evolution of the human psyche. A considerable challenge was limiting the number of words and the restricted time allotted for the presentations, which, as Professor Barbieri insisted, must each be self-contained! An exercise in extreme synthesis that has, regrettably, produced some repetition.

But my overall desire is to introduce the reader step by step, year by year, to what a theoretical psychoanalyst, the *only* analyst at these meetings, committed to expanding the reach of our method and theories, had to say. These lectures represent my contribution to a cutting-edge unifying conceptual paradigm through the venue of these communities of scholars, an effort to break into academia while remaining unfettered by its pedantry, bringing fruits from the unique findings of our psychoanalytic methodology.

Anna Aragno PhD

Lecture I Paris
Background and Origins

...the ultimate cradle of biosemiotics rests, if tacitly, in antique medicine.... the earliest Greek theories of signs originating in medical diagnostics... detecting signs of the body that express disease... Codes, in summary as defined by the Oxford and Webster's dictionary consist of a 'systematic set of laws of signals or symbols, whose meaning is arbitrarily chosen, used for secrecy, brevity, or... processing of information.
—*Cobley (2010) citing Thure (son of Jacob) von Uexküll, p. 114*

Abstract

It's 1900, the beginning of a century of enormous upheaval in many areas of scientific knowledge, when Freud bursts in with *The Interpretation of Dreams,* provoking a combination of scorn, wonder, and ridicule. A masterwork of scientific observation, the "dream book" marks the birth of a research method, insufficiently appreciated then as now. Through deciphering the grammar and syntax of a "primary process" laid out in detail in chapters six, and especially seven, Freud arrived at his first *topographical* theory of mind, the cornerstone of psychoanalytic metatheory. Given these initial insights, Freud fervently believed that his theory of dreams held enormous promise for the study of mental evolution. He remained disappointed to the end that the importance of this avenue of investigation was not fully recognized.

In clinical practice we listen to verbal narratives of pictographic elements expressing sensory-affective experiences still tied to perceptual impressions and bodily feelings in the very process of being transformed into ideational re-presentations. These iconic clusters stretch from sensory-kinetic-emotive *physical* experiences, to memories, impressions, fears, and desires. They exhibit proto-semiotic mechanisms of pre-linguistic tropes and cognition, obeying laws that differ fundamentally from those of Aristotelian logic,

9

exposing a "psychic reality" that is idiosyncratic and highly personal. With its metaphorical, manifest/latent structure, the dream is our MRI, a "royal road" into unconscious mentation, as sharp an investigative instrument into the functional/forms of human cognition as can be found.

Nowadays the range of detectable and interpretable unconscious meanings has expanded considerably, thereby increasing self- and conscious-awareness. In the interest of generating an integrative paradigm linking body and mind, this presentation pursues a personal passion; to continue where Freud left off regarding the scientific metatheoretical importance of studying semiotic processes in dreams, viewing these, and the linguistic interpretation of their meanings, as a window into the evolution of epistemologies of the human mind.

* * * *

Beginnings are wonderful! they hold such promise, such élan, and it is a real privilege to be part of this one, especially since, if Vienna was the birthplace of psychoanalysis, Paris was the boudoir of its conception! We gather here to reconstitute a platform for the unifying ideas that guide our shared interests, an interdisciplinary community pulled apart by a fundamental disagreement over what defines "semiosis" in its modern amplified form as a seedling process at the origins of life itself. It is clear, at least to me, that any attempt to impose "interpretation" as the defining criterion for a sign, not only collapses into quasi-absurd anthropomorphizing when applied to molecular processes, but may seriously jeopardize the whole prospect of a universal "biosemiotic" paradigm. A "sign" becomes a sign when we denote some "thing." Not only ought we demand a more precise definition when using any other concept in its stead, but a much deeper understanding of "meaning" must soon follow.

This thornier issue will eventually require a systematized typology defining different *kinds* of meanings and forms of reference, and *how* these are obtained, from codes and signals, all the way to the most conceptually abstract *symbolic* meanings attached to systems of signs that are generated and used only by humans. A universal semiotics will have to account for, and incorporate, many different forms of information-transmission along such a continuum. These areas of study, I would add, have been anticipated and recommended by the finest minds such as A.N. Whitehead, B. Russell in philosophical logic, N. Goodman, in the philosophy of language, and Ogden and Richards in their classic "The Meaning of Meaning," while the general unification of science and the humanities—to which a universal semiotics lends itself—is today advocated by E.O. Wilson.

Regardless of the nature of these disagreements, thanks to T. Kuhn (1962), we understand such ideological rifts to be symptoms of paradigm fracture or disturbance. That this split should have occurred so quickly in so young and newly formed a scientific community, attempting to amplify the study of bio/semiotics, is disappointing, but not surprising. Paradigm shifts implicitly arouse strong resistances, especially from communities with entrenched beliefs tugging regressively at the progressive thrust of those that challenge their doctrines.

Rifts notwithstanding, in his exhaustive dictionary of semiotics, P. Cobley (2010), writes that since the 1920s the field of "semiotics," has spread through interdisciplinary discourse into a "universal" semiotics as the *essential attribute of life*, "The study of biological codes,... nowadays... more commonly designated *biosemiotics*—a term independently coined in recent decades in the US and elsewhere..." (p. 180). A rose by any other name... !! *"plus ça change, plus c'est la même chose"*! The definition of a *semiotic* system in this community is that of two independent worlds connected by the conventional rules of a code, the field of "Code Biology" devoted to *"the study of all codes of life, and in particular of the codes that appeared after the genetic code and before the codes of culture"* (Barbieri, letter to Editor, Nov. 2013; *my italics*).

As a theoretical psychoanalyst, with a background in the arts and humanities, *no knowledge of biology whatsoever*, embedded in the practice of interpretive semiosis, I had to think seriously in order to justify my presence and potential value here. I found it first, in the deep "biogenetic" origins and psychobiological strains of our founding theories. But even more relevantly, in the pictographic language, a special "mode of thought" that, though heavily camouflaged, was decoded and presented by Freud (1900) in his groundbreaking, *The Interpretation of Dreams*. In psychoanalysis, our object of study is the human mind, its conscious and unconscious worlds, a singular mind that is both code-maker *and* adaptor, creator *and* translator of meanings that are hidden and unknown to ourselves. Freud began, and we continue, to deepen this study through a methodology that is primarily a *dialectical dialogue* that generates reflective processes serving, both to look into others' as we simultaneously take ourselves as subjects of study.

Barbieri's model identifies two distinct molecular mechanisms underlying organic codes: "transcription and translation," or copying and coding. These primary mechanisms at the core of life may be generalized and carried over into higher levels of semiosis, particularly to the dream, a phenomenon lying on the border between biological and psychical processes. Accordingly, I operate under the assumption that natural biological coding mechanisms originate and may serve as templates for mental processes, working through the human central nervous system, that are normally associated with cerebral functioning, an inquiry that will involve sensory, mnemonic, cognitive, motor, and emotional systems, all feeding into the multidetermined configurations of dream imagery.

The "Dream," in psychoanalysis, originating source-point of the Freudian metatheoretical cannon, foundational pillar of his first model of mind, and paramount instrument of clinical insight, is regrettably now an undervalued, endangered species in our field. Along with few others, I continue to make special use of it as the crowning centerpiece of my practice and theoretical focus. Not even so much for its avenue as the "royal road" to the unconscious, a veritable MRI of a dynamic moment in subjective experience, but for its value in disclosing semiotic meaning-forms that predate, anticipate, and underlie, language, with its linear syntax and restrictive vocabulary. Due to the complexity of the topic, and the many strands of knowledge required to fully understand the extraordinary amount of psychical information contained in "dream codes" (which continues to expand), I will be covering the topic from a variety of historical, theoretical, clinical, and revisionary perspectives, beginning today, at the very beginning,

I am interested in looking for points of continuity between biological and socio-cultural semiotic processes along broad evolutionary lines, as well as social and psycho-cognitive phenomena, an inquiry that requires bold new generalizations superseding separatist traditions. Exposing the roots of natural coding mechanisms and extending this template to higher level signal, sign, and symbol systems, provides a model for a universal semiosis from which to formulate and test hypotheses across disciplines and species. Although semiosis and psychoanalysis share common roots in ancient diagnostics, they have, strangely, developed in separate domains; I will be tracing the course of the path by which their natural unity is restored.

Today I present a broad historical picture of the scientific atmosphere, especially in areas of medical-neurology and psychiatry, but also in evolutionary biology and embryology, sexology and anthropology, existent at the time that Freud began uncovering unconscious meanings behind symptoms and dreams, insisting that, "in the psychical field, the biological is in fact the underlying bedrock" (*paraphrased*, Freud, 1937, 252) And so to the very beginnings:

Background and Origins

> Biologically dream-life seems to me to proceed directly from the residues of the prehistoric stage of life (one to three years), which is the source of the unconscious and alone contains the aetiology of the psychoneuroses: the stage which is normally obscured by an amnesia similar to hysteria…"
> —*Freud, letter to Fliess, March 10, 1898*

It is autumn of 1885, and the twenty-nine-year-old Freud is here in Paris on a six-month travel fellowship to continue his research in neuro-pathology and study with the great Jean-Martin Charcot at the famous *Salpêrtrière*! In his report to his College of Professors at the University of Vienna, he underscores the large assemblage of valuable material in neuropathology he has found here, and his admiration for Charcot's teachings in the French school's novel approach to hypnotism in relation to hysteria, all new and unfamiliar to him. Now in his sixties, Charcot has been at the hospital for 17 years, and his charismatic lectures, of such "perfect form," Freud comments, dramatic public demonstrations, his dispassionate attention to all comments, along with his flamboyant *soirèes,* draw many young foreign students, infecting them with enthusiasm. Freud becomes an unqualified admirer, partly mesmerized by the accessibility of this "great man" but also swayed by Charcot's belief that the theory of organic neurological disease was complete, and that the real new frontier lay in uncovering the laws behind the mystery of hysterical symptomatology. Arriving on October 13, 1885, a neuro-pathologist, Freud leaves in the late spring of 1886, completely transformed, with a new path, a new passion, a new profession, and a new mission!

While in Paris, he had already written a paper differentiating organic neuro-pathological paralysis from hysterical conversion symptoms that mimic it. He even found time to translate a book of Charcot's lectures, a feat he later repeated in record time when visiting Bernheim in southern France of the "Nancy school" of hypnosis. The facility and speed with which the busy Freud accomplished these copious "translations," is insufficiently noted, a factor that foreshadows his later capacity to decipher, interpret, and transcribe "another," far more obscurely coded language, that of dreams.

Returning to Vienna he joined his teacher the physician J. Breuer in the bedside treatment of the mysterious symptoms of the little understood disease of hysteria, occurring mostly in females. This collaboration yielded the famous "Studies in Hysteria" 1895, in which a preliminary model of unconscious determinants was proposed and a "talking cure" initiated: hysterics suffer mainly from "reminiscences" producing psychogenic symptoms that are compromise-formations. Verbal abreaction with emotional recall seemed at first to obliterate each symptom, one at a time. This was known as the "cathartic" method. Hypnosis was used as a means of overcoming a defensive resistance to tapping memories that were kept "repressed," whose dynamic charge expressed itself via symptomatic signs that contained specific hidden meanings. But relief was only temporary, a more lasting treatment was necessary. As Freud continued developing his "talking method" a preliminary model was quietly taking shape.

This same year, 1895, Freud wrote but soon discarded his "Project for a Scientific Psychology." Peppered with Greek symbols, this was an attempt to construct a neuro-physiological model of mind based on quantitative energic principles that might satisfy the scientific requirements of his exacting medical community. Although there is as yet little of what will unfold through his empirical "method," this early thermodynamic endeavor emphasized homeostatic constancy, placing a pleasure/unpleasure *principle* at the heart of motivation, hence the centrality of the "wish" in fueling dreams. Abandoning these physiological strictures freed Freud to move ahead with his own observation of latent meanings behind the manifest signs of "motivated forgetting," "suffocated affects," and a mind split into conscious and unconscious levels, kept divided by a defensive "repression barrier."

With the seeds of what he was gestating written out in a prodigious correspondence with his influential friend W. Fleiss, Freud settled into his practice and began "listening" in a unique evenly-suspended, non-judgmental, loose way, to a spontaneous free-associative narration by patients who soon began telling him their dreams. Having discovered that conversion symptoms expressed unconscious meanings, he surmised that dreams, likewise, were compromise solutions, resembling neurotic symptom-formation, and that they too held interpretable meanings. In mid-August 1897, Freud began his own self-analysis, a solitary feat in which he labored to uncover memories, conflicts, complexes, and, via elaborate labyrinthine free associations, to interpret his own dreams.

An avid reader and prolific writer, well indoctrinated in the scientific *Weltanschauung* of his day, Freud was at the avant-garde of late-19th-century science and literature, embedded in, and profoundly influenced by, the new findings in human evolution, sexuality, embryology, and neurology of his time. In addition to Meynert, Fechner, and Charcot, Darwin's depiction of life as a struggle for survival, driven by self-preservative and procreative instincts, was an important influence: hunger and sex loom large over Freud's motivational vision, first in a dual-drive theory and ultimately in the abstract "Life and Death" instincts. Other major influences were Jean-Baptist Lamarck's "inheritance of acquired characteristics" idea; Ernst Haeckel's fundamental biogenetic law "ontogeny recapitulates phylogeny" and Stanley Hall's recapitulation theory: J. Hughlings-Jackson's epigenetic neurology and doctrine of psychical "dissolution" of the nervous system, or "regression," in turn, influenced by the evolutionary philosophy of Herbert Spencer: the emergent "sexologists," notably Albert Moll, R. Krafft-Ebing, and Havelock Ellis; and T. Lipps' spearheading the ascendance of developmental/evolutionary approaches in scientific circles.

Against the backdrop of this medley of ideas, Freud begins to shape a truly psycho-analytic model of mind grounded in three fundamental processes: **regression, repression, and the pertinacity of early impressions**. Briefly: there are three kinds of **regression**, topographical, formal, and temporal; in sleep this implies a return to more archaic *modes of thought*, earlier *forms of experience*, and early memories. There are two kinds of repression; primal organic (or natural) repression, acquired over millennia of evolution that predisposes to a secondary *pathogenic* repression, the cornerstone of neurotic misery. The imprinting impact *of early experiences,* because these are not yet re-presented, will yield the theory of infantile "amnesia," of the first five years.

These three central ideas, and the later polarized "Life and Death" instincts, ground psychoanalysis in bio-genetic principles along two causal tracks: the distal-phylogenetic, and proximal-ontogenetic, yielding dynamic processes that fuel the formation of neurosis, jokes, common parapraxes, and, most fundamentally, dreams. With the dream, Freud has moved out of etiology and medical territory, and into that of a normal universal psychical phenomenon, a step that leads directly to his first *general* (topographical) theory of mind. Between 1895 and 1900, Freud has developed a psychobiological model of mind built on a psycho-Lamarckian biogenetic paradigm of human development that will soon also underpin his model of phases in psychosexual development.

Why is this all so important?

Because these key premises, embedded in a dynamic model of a multilevel mind, divided by a repression barrier, are the soil from which Freud identifies the structural properties and motive force of dreams as he deciphers the grammatical/syntactical mechanisms of their primary-process code. These foundational ideas are fundamental to understanding dream structure and the full span of "meaning-forms" that emerge from their compositional processes of signification. In 1900, Freud's *Interpretation of Dreams* was met with considerable scorn and ridicule. Yet it is here, in chapter 7, that the full measure of Freud's current knowledge and powers of observation, translation, and conceptual synthesis, combined with his stalwart independence of thought—all of which have been developing in these five gestational years—deliver a work of inspired insight that, "falls to one's lot but once in a lifetime" (Freud, Vienna, March 1931, Preface to the third Ed., 1900) a work that will impact the science of mind forever.

The Dream, in psychoanalysis, is portal and bridge at the biosemiotic border; a silent gateway that telescopes back phylogenetically to earlier, more archaic modes of presentation, acting as a prism that refracts multiple condensed meanings from a palate of current impressions, fears, desires and problems, as well as backwards, ontogenetically attaching its emotional impetus to fragments of personal memories and experiences from early childhood. In a two-tiered structure the dream-code's grammatical form and vocabulary are created by condensation, displacement, reversals, and symbolic details, through distorted perceptual snapshot-composites of places, events, and characters from the distant past and present, forming pictographic elements in a narrative woven from sensory-emotional cloth, a "*psychic reality*" more powerful by far than reality itself. But every dreamer creates an idiosyncratic private vocabulary for the elements of *content* so that only the dreamer's many personal associations will lead to its hidden meanings and core ideas.

Yet something important is missing...

What is missing is semiosis: although works on symbolic forms were certainly available at the time, only a short inclusion of symbolism, attributed to W. Stekel in the 1911 third edition of the Dream book, appears in Freud's writing. This is because its study was then the province of metaphysics and philosophy, not yet within the purview of a scientific psychology. Furthermore, Freud was intent on strengthening, not loosening, the biological foundations of mind as a "bulwark" (his word) against mysticism. Yet the dream as another "mode of thought" remains stubbornly obscure without a semiotic analysis; it emerges from less, even undifferentiated, proto-semiotic recesses of human experience, where language has yet to penetrate or assign significance to what *has already been apprehended by the senses and cognition.* It turns P. Bissouaic's statement, "meaning makes sense" upside down, as in dreams it is "the senses that make meanings." By unlocking the key to their interpretation within a discourse-semantic of unconscious forms Freud's methodology opened a window into the evolution of the epistemologies of the human mind.

To be continued...

Lecture II
Deciphering the Language of the Deep Unconscious

Behind the childhood of the individual we are promised a picture of a
phylogenetic childhood—a picture of the development of the human
race,... we may expect that the analysis of dreams will lead us to a
knowledge of man's archaic heritage, of what is psychically innate in him.
Dreams and neuroses seem to have preserved more mental antiquities
than we could have imagined possible: so that psycho-analysis may
claim a high place among the sciences which are concerned with the
reconstruction of the earliest and most obscure periods of the beginning
of the human race.

—*Freud, 1900, p. 549*

Abstract

After garnering a reputation as outstanding research biologist, neuro-
pathologist, medical theorist of the etiology of hysteria, and even
Cocaine experimenter, Freud now daringly applies his cumulative clinical
observations and interpretive acumen to decoding the pictographic language
of the common dream. *The Interpretation of Dreams* (1900) elicits a
combination of wonder and considerable skepticism in a Viennese medical
community not uniformly swayed by Freud's psychical turn. Working in
his legendary "splendid isolation," Freud has produced a masterwork of
scientific observation which, in chapters six and seven, presents a detailed
analysis of the two-tiered structure, the motive force, the formal properties,
and compositional grammar and syntax, of a "primary process" vocabulary,
the deeply unconscious language in which dream-meanings are spun.

He has arrived at these landmark observations, and *a scientific method
of interpretation*, through the conceptual syntheses of the biogenetic law, the

unconscious as phylogenetically archaic; the primacy of early experience; the power of repression and formal regression in sleep; a process he called the "dream-work;" and, most importantly, the sharply dichotomized "primary" (impulsive) and "secondary" (inhibitory) processes, as cognitive *principles* of mental functioning. Couched in his first *topographical* model of mind (Ucs. Pcs Cs), the cornerstone of psychoanalytic metatheory, with the *Interpretation of Dreams,* Freud establishes himself as the fountainhead of a general dynamic psychology.

Here, I cover in detail the mechanisms of the dream's "primary process"—the actual code of dreams—and the "dream work" as laid out in chapter seven of the dream book. However, the dream's manifest-latent structure, the various mechanisms of the "primary process," the "dream-work," and its "secondary revision," I suggest, reveal a precursor underlay in human cognition of proto-semiotic forms, exhibiting modes of meaning-making in *statu nascendi,* only subsequently shaped into linguistic tropes and linearized through syntax and narrative form. I will, therefore, conclude with an eye toward a more contemporary, biosemiotic re-vision of some basic Freudian premises, updated through an interdisciplinary palate composed from neurobiology, semiotics, linguistics, dialogics, and narrative theory.

* * * *

I pick up where we left off in Paris, and, once again, cover the topic from a variety of historical, theoretical, and clinical, perspectives. Today I focus specifically on Freud's unveiling of the structure, vocabulary, motive force, and interpretive technique, of the common dream, as presented in chapters six and seven of his seminal "dream book" (1900), marking the birth of psycho-analysis.

By the end of the 1800s Freud, now married and settled in a full-time practice for neurotic disorders, is also busy giving lectures to the Viennese medical community and growing increasingly passionately consumed by his new obsession, "psycho-analysis." Within a five-year span of explosive productivity bursting with insights, Freud has already written the core works of his early general model of mind, essentially putting the human unconscious on the map, announcing to the world that we know far less of ourselves than we ever imagined, and that, more often than not, we are fueled by primitive drives and impulses we completely disavow. His therapeutic "method," ever evolving via emendations, was proving to be a viable source of income and even richer source of material for the researcher in him since, for Freud, *direct clinical observation* was the only truly scientific approach.

Nevertheless, in deriving his theoretical models, Freud was influenced conceptually by his neurological background and the cutting-edge topics of his day concerned with origins, early development, sexuality, and especially Darwinian naturalistic/evolutionary ideas. Had he written nothings else— with *Studies in Hysteria* (1895) the *Interpretation of Dreams* (1900), *The Psychopathology of Everyday Life* (1901), the "Joke book" (1905), and *Three Essays on the Theory of Sexuality* (1905)—by 1906, the theoretical foundations of psychoanalysis had been laid down. Freud's scientific interest in the dream as *mental phenomenon,* however, had sparked early on, ten years before, during the treatment of Frau Emmy von N. (Breuer & Freud 1893–1895) who spontaneously described her dream-life. Once Freud had abandoned hypnosis, his patients' copious, often effusive, dream narrations became the starting point for the method of "free association" as a way of reaching core unconscious *ideas* that are responsible for symptoms and dreams alike.

Let me begin by giving you a sense of the scope of Freud's dream book: in over seven hundred pages, it covers volumes four and five of the twenty-three volumes of Freud's complete works in *The Standard Edition*. He begins swiftly by presenting his interpretive method, offering the analysis of his own July 23–24, 1895, now famous "specimen dream," of Irma's injection (p. 107) demonstrating, through painstaking labyrinthine associations, how he arrives at its core "meaning" as well as his theoretical understanding of dream structure. Punctuated by many other illustrative dream-samples, there follow chapters on the dream as wish fulfillment; its distortions, sources, and material (including somatic, infantile, recent and indifferent, stimuli); its affective and intellectual aspects; and its crucial manifest/latent structure, arriving, on page two hundred and seventy-seven, to the core "dream-work" and its four key formal mechanisms (of which we will hear much more). Organized in subsections, we are then presented with the decoding of the syntactic-compositional and psychological processes of a pictorial grammar telescoping different types of memory, engaging imagination, sensory/ kinetic-sensations, emotions, infantile drives, perception and language, a visual-spatial *expressive* cognition fueled by a "wish," that he defines simply as "another mode of thought" (p. 541). According to Freudian metatheory, this form, and its characteristics, are a precursory way of "thinking" that persists in the unconscious. In fact, for Freud, the dream's mysterious, other-worldly, pictured-rendering, is merely the transformation of its core ideational content into sensory imagery.

In taking up the unprecedented task of "investigating the relations between the manifest content and the latent dream-thoughts and of tracing the processes by which the latter have been changed into the former (p. 277), Freud (1900) reveals that the dream's core thoughts are transformed into pictographic dream-narratives by a "highly complicated activity of the mind" (p. 122). He called this "the **dream-work,**" an impartial process that "restricts itself to giving things a new form" (p. 507). At this time, however, neither what this activity is, nor its primary operative functions, were understood as *semiotic* processes, nor, therefore, could these be integrated logically into the body of psychoanalytic metatheory as explanatory for its practice and cure.

Nevertheless, Freud's analysis of its component "mechanisms" yielded the following structure: "The dream-thoughts and dream-content are presented to us like two versions of the same subject-matter in two different languages: the dream-content seems like a transcript of the dream thoughts into another mode of expression..." (p. 277). This transformation is effectuated by four mechanisms of the unconscious "**Primary Process.**" These are: **(i) Condensation**: dreams are a mass of these composite, multidetermined, polyvalent, images and elements: **(ii) Displacement**: here one person or object is displaced onto, or taken to represent, another; for Freud this would be in the service of camouflage due to super-ego "censorship": **(iii) Means of representation** (or considerations of representability) i.e., idiosyncratic signs, universal symbols, *pars pro toto* (synecdoche), metonymy, analogy, parody, reversals, all kinds of embodied, organic, dimensional, geological, geographical, meteorological, spatial, and architectural metaphors ("as if," and "if then," relations). In particular, Freud mentions the "just as" relation of similarity, consonance, or approximation, as being "highly favoured by the mechanism of dream formation" (p. 320) stressing that "instances of 'just as' inherent in the material of the dream-thoughts constitute the first foundations for the construction of a dream" (p. 320), a point to which I will return: and (iv): the **Secondary**

Revision, a storying form of narration, or "sense-and-sequence-making," evincing the infiltration of ordering, linearizing processes belonging to the linguistic **"Secondary process"** mode of thought. Together these generate the dramatic, typically bizarre, phenomenalistic experience and account of dreaming.

Confusing manifest content with latent meaning would mean missing the entire process of the "dream-work," considered the *fundamental unconscious "labour' of mind,"* referred to as the "mind's work" elsewhere. Freud (1900) recommended not underestimating the contribution to core "dream-thoughts" of the reappearance in the "sensory image" (p. 547) of the distant past from infantile/childhood. This occurs when memory of an early experience is rekindled by the current "day residue" which functions like a stimulus-trigger—a metonymic hook—connecting early, emotionally charged experiences, with current impressions. Whereas dreams normally conflate past with present, they may also substitute for "remembering" by reproducing infantile scenes that have been *"modified by being transferred on to a recent experience"* (p. 546), pointing to the pervasive role of both unrepresented and repressed memories in the overall "transfer" basis of dream structure.

Language is not absent in dreams but when it appears, is conspicuous. presenting as an isolated statement, a voice, an aphorism, or, as in Freud's famous rebus-like puzzle. Puns abound belying the underlying cross-modal weave of human cognition. And the dream's synesthesia exemplifies how input from all senses merges and converges in the creation of composite images signifying, but also *signified by*, multiple meaning-forms. Two such fundamentally different kinds of semiosis are best understood according to Langer's (1942) distinction between *presentational* and *discursive* form. Dreams contain all types and levels of semiotic organization; signals, signs, and symbols intermingle, cross-referencing meanings that are composed of aspects of all three. These distinct semiotic forms appear unequally distributed depending on the kind of dream, the degree of its affective charge, and how well its core ideas are re-presented, providing ample diagnostic clues as to the state and development of the semiotic function, the capacity to contain affects, and overall personality organization. And while it has been argued, even by those who believe psychoanalysis belongs in the realm of semiotics (Edelson 1972), that the dream's deep structure parallels Chomsky's deep structure of grammar and is in fact *dependent* on language, in agreement with Freud, I believe quite the opposite to be true: the dream's pictographic meaning-code probably antedates language phylogenetically, *prefiguring* linguistic tropes, while ontogenetically, the ability to construct the internal image—and "object constancy"—go hand in hand with naming and the beginnings of language acquisition. The mental image obeys laws of *conceptualization* rather than perception-proper, a point that validates Freud's insistence on the *ideational essence* of dreams. This implies that there are *ideas without words* and that cognition is not contingent *on,* but only channeled *through*, the linguistic prism. Moreover, figurative symbols are inadequately represented by language: linear thought may be governed by linguistic form but intuitive sentience is not: it can be pictured, mimed, danced, sung, or dramatized.

The actual storying of its elements belongs specifically to the "secondary revision" which operates under the constraints of linguistic sequencing and a common vocabulary. Here too, not only the dream's narrative-potential and elaboration are significant, but also the way in which it is recounted provide ample evidence for personality style, organization, and the relationship between primary and secondary processes, significant for the ability to distinguish between fantasy and reality. The value of the secondary revision, however, is not only in its communicative shared aspect but also in the benefits of its, often copious inclusion of descriptive asides and linkages pointing naturally to contiguity by virtue of the "and then" of the storying mode. Yet, in and of themselves, dreams are not "narratives" truly formed but disjointed, segmental, disorganized, individual pictured-scenes. A word might be said here about coenesthetic perception and the nightly effort to assimilate a daily deluge of swiftly passing incoming stimuli, perhaps, a way of understanding the metabolizing, organizing, and accommodating function of our dream-life. Dreams being self-referential to an extreme, in this sense, also serve as a private outlet to preserve psychical integrity or equilibrium.

It is important to keep in mind that Freud's uncovering of dream formation, structure, and technique of interpretation, in fact, the entire framework of this 1900 unveiling, falls under the umbrella of his first theory of mind for normality and pathology, the "**Topographical model**," consisting of three systems; *Ucs, Pcs, Cs* (unconscious, preconscious, conscious) overarching the **Primary** and **Secondary Processes**, his two "**Principles of Mental Functioning.**" At this time, Freud's model was of a mind in conflict, *Cs* and *Ucs*, divided and kept apart by a "repression barrier." His dynamic "psychical apparatus" has fundamental "directional" excitatory and motivational qualities accounted for by fictive quantities of "energy investment and expenditure" that change forms, as operative principles. Freud has achieved theoretical cohesion by redressing in psychological terms a neurological concept that has long since had its happiest hour and needs to be superseded by *functional processes,* that of a fluid "instinctual energy" that changes form in moving from unconscious to conscious mental processes: free and unbound in the "primary-process;" delayed and bound by the "secondary-process." Key characteristics of these two ***"Principles of mental Functioning"*** are: the **Primary process** (*Ucs)* that operates via the most expedient path to wish-fulfilment with unbound, loose, and mobile energy; its expressions are idiosyncratic, free, impulsive, simultaneous, paradoxical, irrational, knowing no Time, logic, negation, or reason. The **Secondary process** (*Pcs-Cs*) is linear, sequential, logical, reasoning, operating with delay, within reality and Time constraints, accordingly, with "bound" energy that makes use of verbal "signs." The former faces inward, the latter outward. Whereas the dream may be an uninhibited private egotistical flight of fancy, in its recounting, linguistic constraints and, perhaps, some inhibitory social or moral propriety may result by some of its content being withheld or altered.

Another important feature of this early *Ucs-Pcs-Cs* model is its implicit epigenetic structure, the idea of "regression" to earlier modes of functional organization, dynamic fixation points, and a propensity in decompensation and sleep, to regress toward these; detaching from "reality" in psychosis while returning to an "earlier mode of thought," in dreams. Three distinct forms of regression are identified: (a) *topographical,* implying a regression to "primary process" and the deep unconscious; (b) *temporal,* referring to a return to the distant and recent past, capturing fragments of sensory/affective, unrepresented, as well as eidetic-memories; and (c) *formal*, whereby a return to earlier more "primitive" iconic modes of *re*-presentation have replaced linguistic "secondary process" signs. These regressions typically occur conjointly since what is older in time is more primitive in form, and topographically lies closer to the perceptual end (Freud, 1900, p. 548). Topography is *not* to be taken literally, however, having nothing to do with anatomy but referring to "regions in the *mental apparatus* wherever they may be" (Freud 1915, p. 175). It will be for Piaget to identify that the first "sensory-motor" (unrepresented) stage in cognitive development is actualized and registered in the sensing-*moving body* (Freud's "body ego").

While dreams are considered regressive phenomena, their internal workings "abnormal," akin to pathology, they are also viewed as a normal, universal, unconscious "mode of thought." The dream, then, is a creation constructed out of mental "work," *as well as* a turning back of an "idea" into a sensory-pictographic script, so that "In regression the fabric of the dream-thoughts is resolved into its raw material" (Freud, 1900, p. 543) towards the perceptual end. This material has been gathered and assembled from bits and pieces of fragmentary input from all sensory modalities in recent and past experiences, both important and trivial; it has rekindled early affects and memories fitting and matching select features and qualities of these to current situations and vice versa; it has found connections and forged new unities forming composite, highly condensed images and multidetermined, polyvalent dream-segments; it has sought parallels, similarities, comparisons and analogies through which to point to new dynamic patterns, much as do metaphors (a point to which I will return): and, it has been linearized and narratized in a "secondary revision" while being transfigured into linguistic form during its recounting.

The dream-sphere is a realm that knows no contradiction or negation, an intense non-linear realm of simultaneity that ignores the pull of gravity, knows no limitations of Time, space, distance, or logic, where everything means many things all at the same time (multi-determination or poly-valence) and many forms of meaning are utilized. Once equipped with a dictionary for the depictive vocabulary of dreams, we find ourselves in a world of graphic intensity where soaring emotions and complex abstractions stand side by side with pure childlike wish-fulfilment; things swell or shrink, people appear or recede according to their subjective import; where size depicts status and valence and camouflage is as common as conflation of past with present; where fears are all terrifying and happiness always elation, every image revealing knowledge rejected, denied, or incomprehensible to its creator! Here, siblings and sensations turn into insects and creepy creatures; emotions are tsunamis or typhoons; moods manifest in dark or sunny days; complex ideas form coded equations; interpersonal dynamics reveal their starkest truths; and loneliness or ecstasy, alike, take us to the stratosphere.

But for our current purpose what is most important regarding the early Freudian framework, and the centrality of the dream within it, is his insistence on incorporating the biological underlay into the functional principles of his "metapsychology" (1915), so named to define "speculations about the origin, structure, function, etc., of the mind, and the relation between the mental and physical" (*Webster's New World Dictionary*, 1966, p. 925). Freud labored to create a somato-psychical framework in which the "Unconscious" (Id) was also the "core-self" of an organism governed by a sensitive nervous system that developed to tame, mold, and socialize, what is universally recognized as "human nature." His primary investment in "the mighty primordial melody of the instincts" (1924, p. 62) reflected a need to construct a psycho-biological metatheory accounting for human motivation and behavior, as universal as it could be. But the difficulty of incorporating into the psychical what is instinctual in human nature was compounded by ignoring the primary function of the human brain which mediates action, emotion, and thought, through the socializing use of *sign*s.

For Freud the organic/somatic underlay *was* the true unconscious; "The physiological substrate does not end once the psychical begins but rather creates a psycho-physical parallelism a 'dependent concomitant'" (1915, p. 207). For this reason I emphasize continuity with the body and epigenesis as principles in the origin and evolution of mind. Nowhere is this continuity between biological and psychical more clearly expressed than in dreams which form a "bridge" in a hierarchy from one into the other. Yet without genetic epistemology or the theoretical inclusion of semiotic mediation the fundamental continuity between body and mind, and therefore the translation from unconscious to conscious modes of thought (as well as therapeutic efficacy), are left mired in physicalist metaphors. Freud's reaching for spatial, energic, and economic metaphors to depict formal and functional transpositions in psychical organization were ingenious constructs through which to grasp the multilayered, polysemic, transformative potential of a *sign-infused* psyche.

Although he artfully interwove biological drive with mental representation through the motivational "wish" as propulsive impulsion, the underlying clash between the universe of *causal explanation* versus *interpretative understanding* was not mended, since meaning is not *caused* but *created*. With characteristic insight Freud bitterly lamented the *Weltanschauung* of his day that it did not provide adequate conceptual tools for his discoveries. The paradigm his life's work was pointing to would not materialize until the fifties with studies in the development of the semiotic function and "cybernetics," a "living" paradigm of pattern, form, and inter-systemic *in*formation. With ample corroboration from neuroscience, it is now commonly accepted that emotion and reason, affect and cognition, are intimately connected: the biosemiotic underpinnings implied in Freud's models needed updating, their grounding in biological affects and drives, modernized, not abandoned. Nevertheless, the implicit plasticity and epigenetic composition of Freud's topographical model provides important inroads into the early roots of mind through its directional features and the types of regression it identifies. A more fleshed out biosemiotic developmental model of mind (Aragno, 1997/2016), built on the skeletal outline of Freud's tripartite topography, composed of micro-genetic developmental steps and stages towards symbolization, undergirds evolution, ontogenesis, and clinical dialogical progressions from unconscious expressions to conscious understanding. With Barbieri's (2015) comprehensive development of a code-based paradigm seamlessly connecting molecular-organic codes with neural and cultural semiosis, we are now in a position to establish logical continuity between micro- and macro-evolutionary processes of mind. The generative templates of nature, copying-and-coding in Barbieri's paradigm, I will propose, apply to the dream which may, in fact, provide a window into this pivotal transition from organic to neural process.

Of one fact Freud (1900) remained certain to the end: the "primary process," he maintained, is present from the beginning, and represents the core of our being, while the "secondary process" overlays it only gradually in the course of development. His confidence in his analysis of dream structure and its exceptional value as an instrument of research was enduring, convincing him that psychoanalysis must command a high place "among the sciences concerned with the earliest most obscure periods of the beginnings of mind" (p. 549).

In summary: This presentation has covered the mechanisms of the "primary process"—the actual dream codes—and the "dream work" as laid out in chapters six and seven of Freud's dream book. These ground-breaking theoretical novelties cluster around Freud's integration of the two *Principles of Mental Functioning* with the three *Systems* of his "Topographical" model,

(Ucs. Pcs. Cs.). Together with primary and dynamic repression, these core precepts represent the *foundational principles* of early psychoanalysis. However, the dream's manifest-latent structure, the various mechanisms of the primary process and particularly the function of the "dream-work" —to *give*-form—reveal a precursor underlay in human cognition of proto-semiotic forms, exhibiting various modes of meaning-making in *statu nascendi* only secondarily shaped into linguistic tropes and linearized by narrative form. Elsewhere (Aragno, 2009), I proposed viewing the dream as *metaphorically* structured, discussing why Freud, who explicitly emphasized its manifest/ latent and transfer structure, missed defining its overall *metaphorical* form. For its importance as primary cognitive instrument, preeminent vehicle of novelty, and its relevance in reconstructing the origins of mind, I will return to this crucial point in detail.

To be continued...

Lecture III
Meaning's Vessel:
Metaphor, the Matter of Mind

...dreams are nothing more than a particular form of thinking made possible by the condition of the state of sleep. It is the dream-work which creates that form, and it alone is the essence of dreaming—the explanation of its peculiar nature.

—*S. Freud 1900, p. 506f*

Abstract

Alone in foreseeing the potential implied by his decoding of the language of the unconscious, Freud (1900) believed his dream book provided propositions from which "a number of inferences can be drawn that are bound to transform our psychological theories" (xxiv), holding enormous promise for future research. Yet already in the preface to the second edition (1911) he laments the general lack of recognition of the importance of these insights.

Despite many writings about dreams in clinical psychoanalysis, no scientific advances beyond Freud's have been proposed regarding how the theory illumines the source-point, evolution, and accretion of representational and semiotic forms unique to the human mind. I too believe the dream holds a key to unveiling the prehistory and evolutionary ascent of human mentation and, through language, to conscious awareness. The development of these ideas, however, required some revision and expansion of the model of mind in which Freud was operating in 1900 and a brief discussion of the epistemological framework.

The dream's compositional structure and formal primary process mechanisms reveal the multi-sensory-motor and emotive sources from which both presentational and denotational semiotic systems originate.

Though expressed in embodied pictographic form, the primary fabric out of which human *meanings* are generated, the dream's signifying mechanisms, are precursors to linguistic tropes and more abstract semiotic systems. The linguistic interpretation of dreams, negotiated contextually through dialogue in a semantic of the unconscious, further unveils the translation from primary to secondary process as the unconscious is made conscious.

The central thesis in this presentation rests on revisiting the cognitive implications of Freud's theoretical analysis of dreams: What Freud called the "Dream-work," exhibits in *statu nascendi* proto-semiotic processes within an overall *Metaphorical* structure, expressing unencumbered personal wishes, fears, and current concerns. Why, then, did Freud not call this structure by name? I will propose an explanation while examining the implications for human cognition of the dream's embodied metaphorical structure in light of contemporary understanding.

* * * *

Meaning rules human action, whereas cause determines physical processes. The rules of meaning rather than the laws of nature explain human behavior.

—E. Hutten, 1981 (in Pines 1981, p. 277)

I pick up where I left off in Jena, continuing my inquiry into the connections between body and mind with the dream—a bridge between biological and psychological—as my entry point. Last year I suggested that the dream's manifest/latent structure, its various primary-process mechanisms, and particularly the function of Freud's "dream-work"—to *give-form*—reveal a precursory underlay of meaning-making mechanisms exhibiting various proto-semiotic forms in *statu nascendi,* secondarily adopted by language as linguistic tropes. This presentation slants towards the theoretical as these processes are examined and accounted for in a revised psychoanalytic/ biosemiotic model of mind.

We have seen how Freud's 1900 uncovering of the dream's two-tiered manifest-latent structure and decoding the vocabulary of the Unconscious revealed four principal mechanisms composing pictographic imagery. This visual language he called the "**Primary Process,**" its main meaning-making mechanisms, **condensation, displacement,** *pars pro toto,* **simultaneity, pictorial representation,** and **symbolization** contrast with the **"Secondary Process,"** which is tied to language. Freud referred to these as "two principles of mental functioning.'

While Freud's predilection for dichotomizing is a staple of his theories and view of human nature (Ego *vs.* Id, affects *vs.* reason, Life *vs.* Death instincts) he also suggested continuity between Ucs. Pcs. and Cs. systems, a continuum, even, between Id and Ego. And when all is said and done, he concluded, the dream's mass of composite forms is merely "another mode of thought". This sensory-motor-emotive cognition reigns unrestrained in dream life as in Art. Its various constitutive mechanisms, Freud called the "Dream Work" later, referring to them more generally as the "Mind's Work." The dream's latent thoughts are transformed into the manifest content by this "highly complicated activity of the mind," (Freud, 1900, p. 122) a transformation that is effectuated by the above-mentioned primary process mechanisms secondarily sequenced in verbal narration. My goal today is to update and integrate Freud's "Dream/Mind's work," now understood as *signification,* the *constitutive/cognitive* process of "mentation" producing meanings by the human mind.

The psychoanalytic technique of dream interpretation is based on Freud's (1900) conclusions regarding dream structure which, in turn, emerged out of his first "topographical" model of mind (Ucs. Pcs. Cs.). His analysis of its component mechanisms yields the following structure: "The dream-thoughts and dream-content are like two versions of the same subject-matter in two different languages.... or a transcript into another mode of expression..." (from p. 277) creating the bizarre, phenomenalistic quality of dream imagery. We ought not underestimate the infiltration of infantile/childhood experiences into the core "dream-thoughts": this reappearance of the past in "sensory images" (p. 547) is due to the day residue functioning as a trigger—a metonymic hook—connecting early embodied experiences to current impressions, a condensation that conflates past with present. Dreams may also replace "remembering" by replaying infantile scenes that have been "*modified by being transferred on to a recent experience*" (Freud, 1900, 546) pointing to the *transfer* basis of dream structure. In regression the "fabric of the dream-thoughts is resolved into its raw material" (Freud 1900, p. 543). This stimulus-material has been assembled from bits and pieces of input from all sensory modalities, rekindling early affects and memories, and matching select qualities of these to current situations; it has found comparisons and parallels, forging new unities and forming composite images expressing both familiar and new dynamic patterns. We trace these images back to their personal sources via the dreamer's free associations, uncovering their multiple meanings.

We now know that this cross-referencing of memories with current impressions from perceptual, sensory-motor, affective, and relational experiences is the cerebral activity of "dynamic schematization" (Werner & Kaplan, 1963). In forming a schema (a represented concept) from a flow of unorganized and swiftly passing, sensory-stimuli, some features are selected, matched, categorized, and funneled into idiosyncratic, newly integrated formulations (ideas). From an organismic perspective this is precisely the bridging juncture between soma and psyche; here the body originates mind through *signifying*—or *meaning-making* activities. Central to this process, which is biased toward finding common traits in dissimilar experiences, is the essential "transcendence of expressive features" (Werner & Kaplan, 1963) inherent in human apperception. In our search for cohesion and comprehension, we *seek* pattern-matching, finding common features and dynamic constellations in our experiences, most especially those that are highly charged emotionally. When something is as yet unnamed or unknown, we summon a visual image, an "embodied/idea," to signify and represent that concept's meaning; this mental act *is metaphoric*. Freud called this process the "dream- or mind's-work;" Piaget called it "accommodation," the second step in assimilation; and in contemporary cognitive-science jargon, this unconscious cerebral activity of sensory integration and imagination is referred to as "conceptual blending" (Fauconnier & Turner, 2002).

Whatever we call it, this organic digesting, distilling, and form-giving process that integrates personal experiences by *transferring the familiar onto what is new is* essentially a **metaphorical** **process** that cannot really be separated from a more general drive to "make-sense-of" *sensory* input (quite literally), i.e., to organize experience by *formulating* it conceptually—by giving it *a form*. In dreams this imaginative shaping is given free rein in the private, silent, condition of sleep; in waking, the sequencing and grammatical constraints of language itself condition what is spoken about. The psychoanalytic method *expressly* dissolves these strictures, subverting conventional dialogue by inviting a unilateral free-flow of associations, thereby reaching a web of surrounding emotions, feelings, and memories wherein are nested the dreamer's core ideas and meanings.

Dream imagery is created out of signifying and symbolizing processes. These cognitive instruments, later adopted more abstractly by linguistic signs, are already present and actively "working" in the metabolization of affects and dynamic-patterns of interpersonal relations; in the matching of present with past while integrating current experiences through metaphorically structured ideas. In the secondary revision of the dream (its recounting), these mechanisms appear through well-known figures of speech. The unconscious shaping of experience we observe in dreams not only makes use of *metaphorizing* and *metonymic* mechanisms (substitution of a feature for the thing) within an overall *semiotic* structure, but also reveals how these expressive primary process forms are made conscious through interpretive activities equipped with a vocabulary to translate Ucs to Cs.

Almost no scientific advances beyond Freud's have been proposed regarding how our theory reveals the source-point, evolution, and accretion of semiotic forms that create meanings unique to the human mind. Despite our privileged panoramic view of unconscious processes afforded by our method, and having long recognized and used a pervasive metaphoric underlay in dialogue and dream interpretation, scientific progress has come, rather, from the cognitive sciences. There are multiple reasons for this which will unfold in my discussion below. Suffice it to say that what was needed was a revised model of mind (Aragno, 1997/2016), built on the tripartite foundations of Freud's topography, while reconceptualizing and expanding it. The development of these ideas necessitated an updated and modernized revision of the model of mind in which Freud was operating in 1900, a brief discussion of the epistemological framework of which follows.

We may well wonder how it is that Freud (1900), who so fruitfully identified the functional elements of the "dream-work," especially in creating "fresh parallels," (p. 320), deciphering its grammar and syntax; who repeatedly pointed to mechanisms finding "similarity, consonance or approximation—the relation of "just as," (p. 320) in the dream *thoughts* as the foundation of dream construction; and who so frequently implied its metaphorical structure, yet never referred to it by name! Not only did Freud emphasize how central this matching mechanism was in dream formation

(p. 31) but he even recognized the foundational merit of its metaphorical structure: Why, then, did he not call it by name?

There are several possible answers: (i) In Freud's day metaphor was firmly ensconced in a linguistic context, viewed as a figure of speech, a rhetorical or poetic devise. He was looking at unconscious processes that create nocturnal *pictographs,* fundamentally *non-linguistic* processes. (ii) His observations were embedded in a deterministic scientific paradigm requiring that he provide a *causal* basis for observed phenomena. When isolating the various functional mechanisms of the primary process, his vision of the overall structure was conditioned by the need to account for the dream's ***motive force.*** And finally; (iii) as a pioneer in the uncharted terrain of the unconscious, Freud was himself immersed in metaphorical processes in naming new phenomena, becoming a conduit between the invisible and its first "formulation" through a language in which he was the first observer. Functioning as interpreter of the unconscious, our master "metaphorizer" of mind would not have recognized the pervasive workings of *metaphorical thought* underlying dream structure while focusing on its formal elements and purported purpose—to *fulfill a wish.*

We would not presume the mind's "work" to be an empty exercise! Yet the "motive-force" for this phenomenon appears to be ***its own operative processes***: And a "mode of thinking" is not a force, a motive, or a purpose, but a *function* of how the human nervous system and brain "work." This, however, does not provide an explanatory answer for *why* we dream. Freud's recognition that the "dream-work" is simply another mode of thought created a theoretical dilemma that he solved by introducing desire, the "wish," as explanatory spark. He had actually opened the door to an entirely new epistemology of *meaning* that did not fit the physicalist causal paradigm of his day.

Freud's dilemma in facing the scientific community was that while it was considered essential to coin explanatory theories in terms of *"causes, "* he had found himself travelling into the world of *"meanings."* And meanings are not *caused* but *created.* Not only—they are created and re-created subjectively. To find a compromise that could fit two incompatible paradigms, Freud looked to human motivation and found the universal "wish" straddling both propulsion *and* meaning. This formula, however, when examined closely, does not suit every dream without serious contortions, and neither addresses nor uncovers the key biological/semiotic progression that his account of dream-formation might afford.

Even in practice, this theory encountered its first chink when Freud was confronted with the repetitive nightmares of soldiers suffering from the traumatic war neuroses from the First World War where this "wish-fulfillment" did not hold up so well. He accommodated this anomaly to fit the "wish" theory—perhaps a little awkwardly—as an attempt at *mastering* trauma. So although Freud, well in advance of today's cognitive scientists, recognized this underlying primary-cognition as "another mode of thought," he neither identified nor referred to it as a *metaphorizing process* by virtue of: (a) the necessity to present the unorthodox nature of the phenomena of his observations in as scientific a manner as possible; (b) because metaphor was a rhetorical linguistic device outside the purview of science; and, most importantly, (c) because he had to provide a *motive-force* for dreaming. The most fundamental reason, then, lies in the epistemological limitations of science in Freud's day.

While the Freudian technique of dream interpretation works very well in practice, a wish-based theory today poses a problem. After many years practicing clinical dream analysis, we observe that dreams may fulfill wishes but, more often, are attempting to make sense of experiences, metabolize affects, grapple with relationships, and give *pictured expression* to current preoccupations by *formu*lating their multiple and multi-layered meanings into imagistic/conceptual elements. Dreams gather together subjectively woven ideas; like all metaphors, they seem to know more than we do, having found instantaneous correspondences in the essential features of a pattern that subsumes current and past experiences while painting this newly distilled form into something now *signified*. The "motive force" for this nocturnal cognition is more *and* less than wish fulfillment, appearing rather to be a way of organizing and coagulating the dense and ambiguous, richly nuanced, *experiential* quality of our sensory emotional life—just that.

Most cognition is *re*-cognition. Dreams serve several essential functions insofar as through the amplitude of their connotive abstractions, they are able to re-*cognize* and *represent* a wide range of newly integrated meanings that are ill-suited to a discursive semantic. Language never quite achieves the complexity or subtlety of meanings that dream (and artistic) imagery depict. In this sense we might consider metaphor and metonymy as the ripest most succulent fruits of a hybrid tree combining logical and emotional (or *psycho*-logical) branches of intelligence. It is the flower of this tree in dreams that fructifies all personal meanings. Linguistic interpretations, negotiated contextually through dialogue in a semantic space of the unconscious, unveil the transition from expressive, connotive primary to denotive secondary process thought, as the unconscious is translated into articulate, linguistic representation. The ideational processes involved in dream-formation *themselves* generate the functional, formal, and structural preconditions for subsequent more abstract semiotic instruments. The two most basic templates (both enabled by *condensation* and *displacement*) are re-presentation—to "stand for," and metaphoric conceptualization—finding the familiar in the unfamiliar.

Looking closely, we find that the dream's manifest content, formed out of its primary process mechanisms, is not only or merely a "pictured" signifier for what it signifies—and, hence, **a *semiotic product*—**(in Barbieri's language—an "artifact") but that this fundamental "labor of mind" is a pervasive *metaphorizing* process underlying and permeating *all* human cognition, dreams, and dialogues. To these specific unconscious proto-semiotic activities, I now turn in order to discuss, in *functional* terms, the cognitive processes that were implied but not defined, in Freud's models.

The human brain works as the central nervous system's sorting plant by selecting, filtering, and funneling stimuli through *primary* processes that use various signifying mechanisms to organize sensory *bodily*, experiences. This establishes metaphor and metonymy as pervasive mechanisms of human thought *from the get go*. We recognize these mechanisms as source-points, the precursors of linguistic tropes that become *increasingly disembodied* as they are channeled through learned cultural systems of signs and language. The dream's overall compositional form and primary process mechanisms reveal multiple semiotic forms from which *both* presentational and denotational semiotic systems originate.

Now that the "dream-work" is recognized as essentially formed by ***semiotic processes,*** however, we have entered an entirely new theoretical conceptual domain embedded in a contemporary "information" scientific paradigm.

A viable model of mind must now logically be founded on developmental principles of semiotic progression delineating increasingly mediated forms of Symbolization along an epigenetic continuum that correlates with onto-

and phylogenetic evolution as well as corresponding to contemporary neuroscientific research. I have proposed such a revised *biosemiotic* model (Aragno, 1997/2016) tracing how the biological substrate—which Freud considered to be the *true unconscious*—bridges body into mind by passing through a subjectively pictured gateway mediated by semiotic processes in dreams or, socially, through language and other conventional signs. Supraordinate to this process is **Symbolization**—the dream as pictorial *signifier* for ideas that it *signifies*—accompanied by its indispensable qualifying hand maidens; **metaphor**—the transfer of the familiar onto the new; **metonymy**—a feature or attribute substituting for the "thing" meant; **synechdoche**—a part for the whole; **simile**—corresponding to; and **analogy**—by comparison.

Metaphor, especially, appears to me as *meta-code* for meaning, a nugget of experiential understanding encapsulating a complex synthesis of current sensory registrations matched with previous impressions and experiences. And this is really the crux of the whole thing: metaphor is not only, or merely, a *cognitive* act, it exemplifies a semiotic *impulsion* towards formulation, a passionate intellection that creates a *certain kind* of meaning that does not transmit information but elicits *experiential understanding*. Its comprehension demands collaborative attunement and resonance in envisioning something new. A product of unconscious processing it is the first link between the inchoate and the graspable, a composite of sensory data transformed through "the currency of mind" (Modell, 1997, p. 219). This primary abstraction is a human universal, depicted through the vocabulary, syntax, and elemental grammar of expressive accommodation that composes dreams.

Like dreams, metaphors do not deliver "data" but evoke *insight*, image and concept fused in thought, the one signifying the other, nothing that can be digitalized! No techno-wizardry will ever produce a computer that can spontaneously metaphorize or dream! If we fully understand the implications of the interpolation of the "sign" into mental life we would steer clear of any simplistic neural model assuming a one-to-one correlation between complex mental phenomena and their neurobiological substrate.

Metaphorical thought is fundamental; it antedates the symbol proper and is more abstract and expressive than the sign, yet makes use of signal, sign *and* symbol in ratios that reverse, shifting toward symbolic abstraction as it ascends toward linguistic articulation. As with any functional process, we expect it to have its own developmental line; in fact, it moves along a semiotic continuum from its primary, unconscious ideographic form in dreams, all the way up to the most refined, original, linguistic elaboration when filtered through the poetic imagination. It moves in various directions simultaneously, from the particular to the general and back, outward and inward, bottom up and top down (semiotically speaking) quickening the mind by its fluidity, balancing the real with the conceptual, yet anchoring the sense of both while articulating a dimension of meaning that is impossible to pin down. Like a chord resolution, metaphor is unmistakable yet indefinable. In its amplitude of employment—for it often contains other tropes—the power of metaphor in the creation and evolution of mind cannot be overestimated: a cultural metaphor dispersed persuasively can influence a train of thought swaying collective values and ideals. The right regenerative metaphor is a balm to the soul, assuaging fear and rekindling hope. A good metaphor clings to the senses, rippling through the system, codifying experiences in new and imaginative ways. New realities are thereby envisioned and brought to consciousness (Aragno, 2009). I draw your attention to Barbieri's general concept of the creation of artifacts by biological systems as generating new worlds, to which I see a strong parallel here. Understanding the metaphorical process in dreams does indeed open up a new level of awareness in human consciousness, and hence a new world.

The application of metaphoric thought is so pervasive in human sentience it is not surprising that the psychoanalytic process not only unveils its origins, omnipresence and impact, but, *especially* in dreams, fully exploits its transformative potential. And if it is our intellectual heritage as a first step toward awareness, bridging unconscious and conscious worlds, as vehicles of this process, we employ interpretive metaphors in all aspects of psychoanalytic work. Suffice it to say that metaphor springs from unknowable organic depths as a "master instrument," a metacode of human intellection and understanding. I have come to think of it as source, root, and portal of meaning, from which flow and grow all forms of representation and reference, and hence the origins of mind itself.

Now that we have explored the metaphorical process as the gateway from biological sensory experience to a primary re-presentational ideation of its *metabolized mediation,* we are poised to look further at how the body continues to partake in all linguistic discourse, particularly in the psychoanalytic situation where, by loosening the conventions of normal conversation, we expose the sensory-motor matrix, still alive and thriving, operating vigorously in all human intercourse.

To be continued...

Lecture IV
Cradle of Meanings, Origins of Thought
The Dream as Research Vehicle

The phenomena with which we are dealing do not belong to psychology alone; they have an organic and biological side as well, and accordingly in the course of our efforts at building up psycho-analysis we have also made some important biological discoveries and have not been able to avoid framing new biological hypotheses.

—*S. Freud, 1940, p. 195*

Abstract

Freud's trailblazing 1900 Dream book lifted the dream out of the soothsayer's hands and placed it in the realm of legitimate scientific scrutiny. Not only is the dream in clinical psychoanalysis an MRI of the dreamer's psychic structure, predominant preoccupations, and subjective formulations of these, but it also reveals formal processes that provide hypotheses for research into the evolutionary progress of human thought and language. In fact, the dream in psychoanalysis is a prime specimen and empirical window into human unconscious mental processes, where meanings and cognition take shape.

By unveiling its two-tiered semiotic structure; decoding its pictographic language, identifying its constitutive actions as the "mind's work," and establishing a dictionary for primary-process forms of signification, Freud provided an interpretive vocabulary for the dream's compositional meanings while also pointing to fundamental cognitive underpinnings: the dream is "another mode of thought."

Despite these clearly implied cognitive underpinnings in Freud's topographical model of mind, this contribution from psychoanalysis has not been adequately integrated theoretically or made publicly known.

The psychoanalytic use and interpretive understanding of the continual influence of the body's sensory-affective input on mind as well as through metaphorical underpinnings of thought and speech has gone largely ignored. Consequently, emphasis on the pervasive presence of metaphor and metonymy in the underlay of human cognition and language has come from the cognitive sciences, not psychoanalysis.

This presentation continues my inquiry into the infiltration of body in mind from within the framework of a revised biosemiotic model of mind (Aragno 1997/2016) as it addresses the convergence of psychoanalysis with contemporary cognitive research. Most specifically, I will trace how meaning-forms and cognitive-modes may be seen, decoded, and understood, through dreams, in both Freud's topographical model, insofar as this predates contemporary cognitive research.

* * * *

The dream is a transition point between sensory-emotive, organic, and cerebral processes, and their first presentational formulation; a pictorial bridge between body and mind. Psychoanalysis considers this deep Ucs *as biological*, visible only through derivative behaviors, representations, and signs, all of which express human "meanings." Meaning motivates human purpose, fueling imagination and action. Over the last sixty years or so, many branches of the human sciences gradually converged on the issue of meaning, adopting embedded naturalistic methods in the inquiry of forms of meaning-making. This implied abandoning existing physicalist paradigms since meanings are contextual, humanly co-*created*, not *caused*. Psychoanalysis finds itself fair-and-square at the epicenter of these methodological changes, and the dream, its prime specimen, at the very heart of the originating source-point where body becomes mind.

Today, I hope to illustrate how much may be gleaned from dreams regarding the way the human unconscious works: how sensory impression is transformed into significant image; how we metabolize and organize current experience in relation to the past; picture desires; construct emotionally-fraught, condensed, "image-ideas" in an idiom that is incomprehensible to us when awake, the language of emotional-cognition. In order to do this, however, I need to recapitulate what I've covered before, presenting a brief overview of basic theoretical principles and terms that emerged from

Freud's (1900) groundbreaking analysis of dreams. Without this knowledge, none of what follows can be understood.

To begin, some background: Freud was a research biologist by vocation, a medical-neurologist by profession, and a clinician by economic necessity, but at heart he was an empirical observer, informed by the scientific avant-garde of his day, with a literary gift. The problem is that his subject-matter had never before been named, is ephemeral, and is visible only through manifest symptoms, behaviors, emotions and words, a realm in which the *sign* for what is *signified i*s obscure, multidetermined, and must be ferreted out through "psycho-analysis," a research method for which there was no known scientific paradigm. Psychoanalysis was born of this multi-perspectival approach as three things in one: a research methodology, a model of mind, and a therapeutic modality. This last requires a specialized participant/observer listening stance for its unconventional dialogue, and it is important to know which of these hats one is wearing since this determines how the method is used, guiding what one selects to observe and interpret.

Freud's (1900) uncovering of the dream's two-tiered manifest-latent semiotic structure and decoding of the vocabulary of the Unconscious revealed four main mechanisms composing the pictographic scenarios of which dreams are made. This unruly language characterized by ambiguity and timelessness, devoid of logic or negation, he called the "**Primary Process,**" contrasting it to a linear, logical, reality-based, "**Secondary Process,**" tied to language, naming these the "**Two principles of mental functioning.**" The dream is instigated by the "wish" (today, a vastly expanded concept), is private, subjective, and free, often expressing soaring emotions and kinetic or bodily processes. Its linguistic narration, on the other hand, is public and may exhibit defensive inhibitions, even moral abhorrence. We get around this by inviting copious "free associations" and questioning ever deeper for more associations extending inward into a labyrinth of connected distant memories tapped into by metonymic "hooks," often triggered by apparently trivial recent impressions.

The dream's semiotic regression to pictographic form lays bare earlier modes of meaning-making, providing a window into mental evolution in various ways: **formally**—from secondary-to primary process: **topographically**—from conscious to deeply unconscious; and **temporally**—to an earlier time and mode of thought. The dream's segments are referred to as "elements:" they appear strung together by the march of words and the

45

sequential nature of narrative form, the "and then" of the storying mode, in attempts to attribute sense, coherence, and causality—of which dreams have none!

The psychoanalytic technique of dream interpretation is based on Freud's (1900) conclusions regarding dream structure and construction which, in turn, emerged out of his first *"Topographical"* model of mind consisting simply of three *systems*: Ucs-Pcs-Cs. Twenty-three years later he would establish a second more clinically useful dynamic theory of mind, the *"Structural theory"* consisting of three *agencies*: Id-Ego-Superego. Contrasting the two models; the one describes status along Cs-Ucs dimensions; the other identifies dynamic tensions and compromises between psychical forces. This creates a meta-theoretical bifurcation: psychoanalysis as epistemology—the study of how something is known, calling for a systematization of logical forms (as advocated by B. Russell, 1953); psychoanalysis as dynamic theory of character structure. We shall see later how these two models, along with a background in development and surrounding knowledge pertinent to human psychology help reveal the breadth of condensed information contained in dreams.

Freud called the "highly complicated activity of the mind" (p. 122), by which emotional-ideas become images the **"dream-work"** (the **"mind's-work"** elsewhere) a labor that *transforms* sensory experience into *signified* shape. This is a semiotic process, the four, constituent primary-process mechanisms of dream-composition, **condensation**, **displacement** (*metonymy)*, ***pars pro toto*** *(synecdoche)*, **pictorial representation**, and **symbolization,** a precursor underlay of strictly human **proto-semiotic** *signifying* forms. We recognize these as germinal bodily-grounded source-points that grow increasingly disembodied as they are channeled through a conventional system of signs like language. These macro-evolutionary/developmental processes are recapitulated microgenetically through interpretive activities in the psychoanalytic process, and are best conceptualized within the framework of a revised biosemiotic model of mind (Aragno, 1997/2016) undergirded by traceable semiotic progressions along phylo-and ontogenetic lines. This expanded framework integrates and fuses Freud's "Dream- or Mind's work" with semiotic progressions now understood as *the* formative processes in the origination of mind and increasing consciousness.

46

As part of this revised framework, I have proposed (Aragno, 2009) that the dream's manifest/latent structure is fundamentally ***metaphorical***: from the outset, therefore, I make a distinction between *metaphorical thought*, the underlying process of all human cognition, and "metaphor," its coined product. The most primal manifestation of this metaphorical construct, the dream is a work of imagination and intellection, of figurative and cognitive condensation and expression. Its elaboration may spring from a metonymic spark, one "thing" standing for 'another', or it may begin from the other direction, an idea attaching to a percept in order to be "pictured." Condensation and displacement are inherent in its formation. Recognition of the "mind's work" as ***semiotic process,*** the dream as "another mode of thought," as Freud put it, establishes metaphor and metonymy as primary mechanisms in human mentation *from the get go.* And it is precisely here, around recognition of the pervasive underlying dominance in human cognition of metaphor and metonymy, that modern cognitive science meets psychoanalysis, and the two converge on an interest in meaning-making forms.

Metaphor, originates in the Greek compound ***pherein***; to carry, and ***meta***; over; it is the application of a descriptive to something to which it is not literally applicable (*Oxford Dictionary*, 1958, p. 748). Metaphors transport ideas from one domain of experience to another. Metonymy is the substitution of a feature or attribute for the thing actually meant. Both are prominent in the unconscious ideation of dreams. The classical view of tropes (since Aristotle) as linguistic devices has given way to a modern understanding of metaphor as *the* way we initially articulate new concepts, a common mode of thought, so common, in fact, that it pervades everyday speech, is found in all languages, and is the very stuff of dreams. Lakoff and Johnson (1980, 1993) cognitive linguists, who have done for the study of metaphor what Freud did for the study of dreams, assert that "... our conceptual system is metaphorically structured ... most concepts are partially understood in terms of other concepts" (1980, p. 56). They wonder if we are even capable of conceptualizing anything without the assistance of metaphor.

Like narrative, dialogue, and emotional intelligence, a burgeoning interest in metaphor and metonymy has legitimized serious study of what were once afforded less than scientific status. Though manifest through language these instruments are no mere linguist frills of rhetoric: when trying to describe something new we turn to metaphor, configuring novelty in terms of the familiar. So intimately bound with unconscious assimilation, accommodation, and creative integration, is metaphoric thought that it is equally at work constructing a theory as in creating a dream.

Notwithstanding the psychoanalyst's privileged exposure to these processes, it is from cognitive science that influential works on metaphor first emerged. This is not to say that our field has been idle on the subject. Yet our static conceptual framework and terminology undermined our broadcasting that the *entire* psychoanalytic enterprise is metaphorical and metonymic, steeped in transferential processes and semiotic activities. The interpretation of the unconscious transforms primary into secondary process thought, a cognitive process. This includes breaking down psychological defenses which distort cognition and impair judgment in many ways. The process by which these are scrutinized under the analytic microscope leads to awareness and working-through, two lengthy preeminently psychobiological/cognitive activities that are the basis for change.

Nevertheless, as a consequence of a gradual slackening of interest in the methodological application of psychoanalysis to the investigation of *Ucs mental phenomena,* the systematic study of unconscious *thought processes* fell to other disciplines. Cognitive science, however, tells us little about the constituent elements of progressive stages in the joint creation of metaphor; its dynamic-emotional sources; the developmental-interpersonal and intrapsychic implications of its dissolution, breakdown, and reconstitution; its close interaction with other symbolic processes, and its complex interface with primary and secondary modes of thought, two poles that maintain reality and fantasy distinct preserving the stability of mental health. Nor does it touch on the pervasive tendency for metonymic misconstruence in relationships (transference), a shibboleth of the psychoanalytic clinical method.

Several psychoanalysts have pointed to the cognitive underpinnings of our method and theories. Others more recently have addressed metaphor and metonymy as part of the primary process. But none focused on their centrality in dreams as *pivotal* cognitive instruments in the transfer of old to new, from body to mind, or as the igniting metonymic spark in the day residue. These insights remained theoretically unintegrated so that as late as the nineties Lackoff (1993) comments, "Neither Freud nor other psychoanalysts have been interested in working out the details of the system of mundane metaphoric thought, though they implicitly recognized the existence of such a mode of thought and have made use of it... as part of dream interpretation... working out the details of the metaphor system has fallen to linguists and cognitive scientists" (p. 85).

Actually, we have come a long way in our studies of metaphor, understanding that our entire enterprise is metaphorical, and since most of our thinking is metaphorically based, the realities we construct are metaphorically structured and understood. Most cognition is *recognition*—for the most part we understand the new in terms of something already known—we pattern-match. Affects, metaphor, and memory, work together. When a word is sought to express something new, we call first on metaphor: straddling two realms of experience, in one instantaneous iconic flash, metaphor fuses word and image, welding two modes of cognition. We understand human expressiveness to be rooted in the body, in emotion, so our attention is peaked by those linguistic forms—synecdoche, metonymy, allusion, and metaphor—coming from the obverse direction that produce symbolic connectives, depictives, descriptives and explicatives, for hidden meanings. These infiltrate the verbal flow, shedding evocative hues on the pallid string of words as subtle shadings of a master palette capture our gaze. Typically, we conceptualize the abstract or difficult-to-verbalize, in relation to spatial, mechanical, especially organic, domains of experience, and define "the nonphysical in terms of the physical" (Lakoff, 1980, p. 59) (the "house" being an overriding metaphor for the self). For those of us who work daily with dreams, immersed in the semantic, primary process, of the unconscious, it seems quite clear that metaphors are conceptual and figurative, and only secondarily linguistic.

While cognitive science and psychoanalysis both study the unconscious, our methodologies differ in crucial ways: research in the analysis of unconscious stimulus-processing in cognitive science relies heavily on verbal reporting, applying verbal formulations to what may, or more likely may not, be linguistic phenomena. Psychoanalytic methodology, on the other hand, is processual and experiential in a *naturalistic* way; our method interprets meanings spun unconsciously that appear spontaneously in the dialogue and relationship, in dreams, and in a free-flowing account listened to in terms of *unconscious* meanings. This puts us in an optimal position to observe the root-origins, development, and interacting functional processes involved in meaning-making, *in vivo*. Moreover, ours is a dynamic multi-perspectival method, engaging both observer and observed at many levels, bringing a far broader range of unconscious phenomena into play for consideration.

Contrasting his theory of conceptual metaphor in dreams to traditional psychoanalytic models, Lakoff (1993) falls into a common error. He assumes that, "The unconscious discovered by cognitive science is... not like the Freudian unconscious" (p. 87), revealing he makes no distinction between the Freudian *topographical* and *structural models* of one single unconscious. Although governed by different operative principles, these reside in different rooms but live in the same house (in which several other "unconscious" occupants also reside!) The cognitive unconscious of cognitive science is *very much* part of our psychoanalytic unconscious, in both Freudian models, wherein perception, emotion, memory, defenses, and cognitive process, cannot so easily be divided.

Fascination with the substratal rests not unreasonably on the premise that all mental processes are in some way reflected in correlate patterns of neural enervation, that the mind is functionally tied to its neuro-anatomical/chemical underpinnings. From its spontaneous activation in dreams to its linguistic form, metaphorical thought appears to engage multiple cerebral systems, interconnecting many functional regions of the brain. Given its multisensory and mnemonic elements, its polysemic juxtaposition of image to idea dipping into the sensory-emotive and biological bowels of the dreamer's mind, metaphors activate vast networks and layers of brain activity. Whether we adhere to Luria's (1973) "functional systems" holistic model conceptualizing brain in terms of "orchestration," in compositional synergy, or we adopt MacLean's (1973) triune brain model, metaphorical thinking would involve occipital, parietal, temporal, pre-frontal and frontal principal units, from limbic to cortical regions. This is because traces of information from visual, kinetic, emotive, linguistic, and various mnemonic systems are integrated and processed in a variety of ways. At first glance, metaphorical thought activates both "evocative" and "long-term" memory, condensing traces from sensory-emotive as well as represented mnemonic sources to formulate meanings that, once adopted regularly in communication, would have produced rapid growth in neural networks and brain density.

Lakoff and Johnson's (1980) present a similar "neural mapping" model in the terminology of cognitive science. While this model accounts for basic neural mechanisms underlying bodily anchored metaphorical thinking and speaking, again, it is inadequate for the kinds of metaphorical progressions that psychoanalysis encompasses. A comprehensive psychoanalytic model would have to account for neurological conditions that inhibit, obstruct, or decompose, and those that recompose, metaphorical thought, as well as consider the Ucs to Cs dimensions of metaphorical productions, from dreams to symptoms, transference to poetry, along the topographical axis. "Rate of processing," a neural factor connected to working-through and insight—two shibboleths of the therapeutic process—is also of interest to us, given that the image takes milliseconds to register (or conjure) whereas linguistic, conceptual thought, takes a lot longer.

Even if metaphorical thought could be traced to firings in certain neural networks, there is one ephemeral, unique and ubiquitous trait of human mentation that is unlikely to be encountered along any neural pathway, and that is the assignment of *meaning*. No matter how much we look, we will not find the mind's signifying "abstractions" in the brain, nor a locus of symbolization or reference, just as we will not find wonder, awe, disgust or indignation, duty, devotion, resolve or resignation, the whole panoply of strictly human sentiments that endow our experience with human *qualities*.

Categorical and abstract thought employ the brain's highest regions, whereas, more primitive centers spark visceral, mnemonic, emotional, and kinetic responses: metaphorical and metonymic dream processes pervade them all suggesting that the dynamic multiplicity of enervations involved is staggering. Consider that neural networks code information through traces forming "multidimensional matrices" (Luria, 1973, p. 284) from which a particular facet is activated whenever this system is rekindled, pointing to the tight composite quality of the human engram. Subjective experience begins in the sensing-moving body; we first take in the world through ears, eyes, nose, mouth, and hands: hence, the first Ego is a body-Ego. Every sense produces its own signifiers. This has particular relevance in the interpretation of dreams. From each of the senses input has been added and stored, and around these layer experiences in close relationships and culture. The sensory-motor "schema" along with its affective-contextual aura is, and remains, a core unrepresented matrix, slowly coated by increasingly differentiated and diverse experiences. Words are acquired so early that they too are embroiled in this primary soil, and when they appear in dreams, may point to very early roots. In addition to this, also layered, are defenses that shape character; and *all* of this, pictured in what is currently pressing to the dreamer, is reflected in a dream.

The power and immediacy of dreams is due to the fact that they still partake of this sensory-motor emotive experience while also making use of sign *and* symbolic re-presentation. Part body, part mind, dream imagery retains and radiates from this sensory/emotive matrix constellating around bodily experience. This is why primary dream metaphors are grounded in directional, seasonal, natural, or organic processes, while dipping into universal visual, kinetic, physical, and domestic experiences shared within a particular culture. Metaphorical thought spans the gamut of representational forms; its strength lies in calling on sensory experience to signify highly symbolic, abstract *ideas*. Metaphorical thought points outward to see inward; transmitted by evocation, an instrument of conceptual insight.

In the interpretation of dreams, we witness not just the transforming of body into mind, but the pervasive presence of body *in* mind, *all the time*. The formative pieces of sensory-imagery are a first expression of emotional/cognition, still awash in the cross-referencing of stimuli of early synesthesia, transcribed into a figurative idiom generated by the condition of sleep. In a sense, the dream (and we see this clinically) is *already* an advanced crystallization of considerable cerebral processing which has accomplished the work of comparing and matching current with past registrations, finding similarities, and composing condensed images that express the underlying thoughts they depict.

At its inception, and in linguistic form, metaphor operates bi-directionally, from percept to concept, idea to image, and back. This brings visual and conceptual, sensory and abstractive, primary- and secondary-process modes of thought into correspondence, producing the distinctive conditions that "point to one thing while meaning another." Everyday language is full of such subliminal evocations while the language of dreams *is entirely* metaphorical. Metaphorical *insight*, however, is obtained only if *we* can endow *metaphorical meaning*. The burden of this kind of understanding rests on the interpreter who must fuse and use both primary and secondary process thinking simultaneously in order to "tune in" to this kind of poetic vision.

52

Dreams are an MRI of the human psyche, an x-ray snapshot of what is *on* and *in* the dreamer's mind, how it is experienced, what is repressed as well as represented, how this relates to the developmental past, and to current issues and interactions, what role or function the analyst appears to be serving, and what defenses are operating in the recounting. Relationships between *form, content, and context,* are *critical* in clinical work. Dreams cut to the chase, exhibiting dominant Ucs felt-ideas and those hidden.

What then does the savvy analyst see through this instrumental in-road to the psyche? What kind of information and how is it uncovered in the interpretation of dreams?

We see first how the dream is remembered and recounted—is it obscured or elaborated, brought as gift or as eager or reluctant assignment, is it intensely felt, well developed, and vividly narrated or, recalled only vaguely, in fragments, recounted reticently, in awkward, disjointed sequences? We see categories and stereotypes through figurative elements, and what characteristics these represent for the dreamer in their unique history and cultural development. We note the transient detail, expressive gesture, shift of tone, changes in body posture, breathing, and movements, as all these point to that "something else" that analyst's pay attention to. Collectively the unmentioned and bodily expressions contribute significantly to our interpretive understanding of the dream. All important is the context which sets the stage: we note the opening scenario, city-landscape, country-landcape, or seascape, day or nighttime, sunny or stormy atmosphere, whether this is a group, a dyad, or family situation, an event or a drama, where the dreamer is situated (walking, running, flying, swimming), experiencing or observing, attacking or fleeing, the task, problem or goal, and what is singled out descriptively by the dreamer. All these reflect mood, drives, and interpersonal and emotional state in relation to desired ends. Important also is whether the dreamer was awakened and if so in what state, by overwhelming affect or an idea?

As the elements unfold in condensed "composite" imagery, now immersed in the evocative mood elicited by the dream, we follow the narrative trajectory unfolding as it points to a surface storyline while signifying deeper unstated ideas. We note how the narrative ends as in its outcome we uncover unconscious beliefs and assumptions, often leading to self-fulfilling prophecies, paying attention to whether these are optimistic or catastrophic, if they lead to a solution or if they wake the dreamer from a nightmare. And we ask for associations as we go along, deeper and deeper in our probing, prompting recall of everyday impressions, events, old memories, all leading into the labyrinthine mosaic of mind.

From a structural perspective, we observe key interruptions and any inhibitory criticism, disparaging judgments (the voice of conscience), expressions of embarrassment or guilt, and note what is omitted (mentioned later) or only half said but implied; how much the recounting masks conflicts and avoids re-experiencing strong emotions; what figurative elements separate body from mind, how choreographed the avoidance is, as all these reveal defenses at work.

From a topographical perspective we note how attuned the dreamer is to their own puns and metaphorical allusions, how readily these are picked up; how easily they can be adopted and tossed around; how smoothly meanings move from preconscious to conscious, or how deeply disguised the characters and attendant emotions are. The exact words of the recounting are important as are gestural expressions, movements, stops and starts, and what is occurring currently in the room, as sign-relations between form/ content/and acting-out are often formidable. Associations will already appear interspersed throughout the session, and first recounting, but the key to dream interpretation is probing for associations, the deeper the better. The art lies in this dialectical exchange; a skill in which questioning leads inward into the vast interwoven network of associations condensed in each element issuing from core matrices that contribute to the composition of each and every dream image.

Summary and conclusion: In demonstrating how much information psychoanalysis finds in dreams, I have focused on their compositional/ cognitive processes, basic metaphoric and metonymic characteristics, and the unrepresented sensory-motor matrix around which all experiences constellate and layer. These metaphorical and metonymic tendencies are so pervasive in human experience, thought, and language, that they appear spontaneously *throughout* a polysemic dialogue that is especially designed to uncover the unconscious. How, and in what ways, psychoanalysis codifies and instrumentalizes these very traits for its interpretive purposes is . . .

To be continued . . .

Joint Lecture V
The Embodied Origins of Linguistic Codes and Psychoanalysis

Anna Aragno PhD and Tulio Rizzini MD

Abstract

This shared presentation between a neuropsychiatrist/psychoanalyst and a psychoanalytic theoretical revisionist, both independent researchers on different continents, converges on a single point: methodology. Freud's decoding the language of the Primary Process through his analysis of signification in dreams opened the door to an inclusive epistemology focused predominantly on the study of the Unconscious. As a theory of mind, a therapeutic modality, and a research method, psychoanalysis demands multi-disciplinary scholarship. Dr. Rizzini's medical/neurological background and Dr. Aragno's in the Arts, Humanities, and Language, are exemplars of the cross-referencing and breadth of interdisciplinarity that has typified psychanalysis from its inception.

In the first part of this presentation Dr. Aragno's bullet points address pertinent information from the philosophy of science and basic distinctions between Primary and Secondary Processes of thought. Her epigenetic developmental model of semiotic forms pertains to the study of the somatic/embodied phylogenetic origins and ontogenetic recapitulation of learned cultural and linguistic codes.

This segways into Dr. Rizzini's summary of forty years of empirical research into the instinctual somatic/embodied origins of language derived from observable gestural/oral coding processes yielding linguistic phonemes. Given the time limitation, Dr. Rizzini's extensive neuro-anatomical research and its vast etymological implications cannot be detailed but may be found fully developed in his books.

The essential convergence in the study of the developmental line of logical semiotic forms (Dr. Aragno) and the empirical evidence of the somatic/embodied origins of linguistic codes (Dr. Rizzini) rests on profound theoretical and clinical knowledge of tried-and-true psychoanalytic principles. Ours is a young science, just over 100 years old, but one that has precipitated seismic changes in its contribution to universal knowledge in the understanding of human nature and the unconscious, where instinctual drives and motivation originate and most cognition takes place.

Psychoanalytic Method and Theory of Mind in Relation to Signification

Anna Aragno

I teorici della semiotica potrebbero` rimboccarsi le maniche e mettere alla prova la loro discplina, affrontando l'interpretazione dell'arte preistorica.

Theorists of semiotics could pull up their sleeves and put their discipline to the test, by attempting to interpret prehistoric art.

—Anati, 2002, p. 68

Psychoanalysis is a theory of Mind, a Therapeutic Modality, and a Research Method, founded on a body of data regarding unconscious phenomena that is observable only through their manifestations. As a methodology it offers innumerable avenues and subjects of research. Here, two psychoanalysts pursue their topics; one on advancing our metatheory of mind, the other on the origins of language. Both, however, converge on the primary vehicle of human mentation and expression: ***meaning*** and how meanings are made. The "dream" in psychoanalysis is our universal prime specimen, occurring when deeply unconscious, gossamer, yet when remembered may be recounted linguistically. Hence, we have a manifest storyline, narrated from pictographic imagery, expressing latent *meanings* originating in core "ideas"—there is no better demonstration of a semiotic trajectory that possibly recapitulates an evolutionary progression.

1. Basic Background; In his Dream book, Freud (1900) decoded the structure, grammar, syntax, and wish-driven motivation of dreams and in the famous chapter seven presented a model of mind —the topographical— with three systems and two 'Principles of Mental Functioning': the unconstrained, fantastical, unconscious Primary Process, characterized by multidetermined condensations, displacements, reversals, timelessness and idiosyncratic symbolism, in contrast to a Secondary Process, tied to language, linear, time-bound, rational, reality-oriented, and restrained. The formal regression to primary process cognition in dreams reveals the synthetic work of various cerebral systems; perception, memory, and re-presented subjective experience, in action. Lovers of the arts will recognize immediately the resonant qualities of *expressive* meanings that are depicted, emotionally inspired, non-verbal, and inferred by evocation, in contrast to meanings that are aligned linguistically, spelled out literally, in designate denotive verbal signs. These are two forms of meaning-making, two different *modes of representation*, in my conception, two distinct *semantic* spheres; one *compositional* and *connotive,* the other *linear* and *denotive,* each using different semiotic vehicles to express different kinds of meanings through different semiotic operations which, Freud conjectured, might reveal an evolutionary sequence.

2. Philosophy of Science; A Paradigm for Interacting Biological Entities. Psycho-analysis was born just before the quantum revolution, and Freud had died before Piaget and the study of infant and child development burst in on the social and psychological sciences. Much changed in the half century after Freud's passing. He left us with metaphoric terms and analogies for his trailblazing observations in the hope that we would deepen his discoveries and explain their functioning in operative terms as new knowledge accrued. Of particular interest to him was understanding how an interpretive dialogue in a semantic of the unconscious designed to increase awareness alters psychic structure, the essence of the talking cure. But no paradigm existed that could accommodate such transforming organizations of minds. Since then, there has been a rapprochement between science and the humanities, with calls from various quarters for an integration of scholarship between the so-called soft and hard sciences.

In the forties, a group of scholars from different disciplines began stirring foundational ideas that proposed a new paradigm for living systems, one quite different from physics and its deterministic requirements based on causal explanations. Engaged in what McCulloch (1965) named the "Embodiment of mind," this group of anthropologists, psychologists, epistemologists and philosophers of science, were elaborating *Cybernetics*, coined by the brilliant mathematician, Norbert Weiner (1948). This new approach proposed ways of looking at *pattern* and *form* as *organization* for a new science of information, ideas further developed by von Bertalanfy's (1968) Systems Theory. Living, interacting systems, could now to be studied at their interfaces in terms of communication and relationships in non-linear recursive patterns; when applied to interrelating humans these would include elements like purpose, emotion, drive, expressive tone, since meanings are all based on circumstance, intent, and contextual frames of reference. Synthetic thinking evolved with the idea that a system's *coherence* occurs through the shifting organization of its internal parts in relation to other systems (Ackoff, 1975) with which it is in constant contact. This, along with advances in developmental studies, the philosophy of language, schools of linguistics and semiotics, the dialogics of the great Bakhtin (1981, 1986) and, importantly, the new Narrative studies, generated perfect soil for a scientific approach not just for the unconscious (cognitive neuroscience leapt on that!) but for the psychoanalytic method itself—"a conversation," the analytic *dialogue.* Psychoanalysis addresses human inter-actions and communication in a dialogue that goes beneath the limen of consciousness and linguistic exchange, establishing connections at regressed and even "unspeakable" levels. What can we learn from this dialogue about human language, communication, and its origins? Dr. Rizzini's research speaks in answer to that question.

3. A Developmental Paradigm for a New General Model of Mind and Communication: Psychoanalytic domains are unique in establishing rules of discourse for the purpose of exploring and understanding many levels of meaning; our "subject-matter"—the whole human organism—addresses transforming organizations of experience and meanings in *interactions.* A science dedicated to uncovering the laws of "meaning" from Ucs to Cs'ness requires a bedrock planted in principles of semiotic evolution and development. Morphological and epigenetic principles of increasing efficiency and complexity along a continuum are fundamental to this *biosemiotic* enterprise. In two books (Aragno, 1997/2016, 2008/2016), I began systematizing such principles of biosemiotic progression via a revised developmental model of Mind and Human Communication in relation to a discourse-semantic that methodologically orients to uncovering *all* unconscious phenomena, especially transformations from primary to secondary process meanings. Multidetermination makes, of every image or utterance, a condensation of many diverse levels and forms of signification, consequently the interpretive potential in any slice of clinical process is very broad indeed. Drive-derivatives and proto-semiotic expressions shadow metaphoric and higher-level symbolic articulation while residues of earlier stages infiltrate and fuse into higher forms. Each contributes to the whole so that differently mediated elements interweave in free-associative accounts making our discourse densely packed with multiple layers of meanings—like a symphonic score.

This density is reflected in my multi-level developmental model of symbolization which systematizes their stratified forms and organizations along evolutionary/developmental lines, beginning in natural affect-Signals, moving to mediated indicative or denotive expressive and verbal Signs, to complex Symbols. The model documents organizing principles of semiotic mediation addressing the dialectics of sender/receiver in each form. It provides a vocabulary through which to identify and refer to each and accords with phylogenetic and ontogenetic development, yielding useful hypotheses.

4. A Very Brief Overview. Disadvantaged by prolonged dependency, the human infant is well compensated by the biological endowment of a highly effective communicative system of eight primary affect-signals associated with widespread glandular, muscular, and behavioural manifestations. The ability to recognize this species-specific basic repertoire of human expressions is phylogenetically inherited through subcortical centres mediated by the autonomic nervous system. Facial expressions are the immediate, observable indications, of organismic states or dispositions, each accompanied by broad physiological responses generating sensori-emotive feedback. Human infants are equipped from birth to communicate inner states via these embodied expressions. Tomkins (1962–1963), along with Ekman (1969, 1979, 1980) and many other "emotion expression" scholars, consider affects to be our primary motivating system, listing and describing eight universal expressions: **1. surprise/startle; 2. interest/excitement; 3. enjoyment/joy; 4. distress/anguish; 5. contempt/disgust; 6. anger/ rage; 7. fear/terror;** and **8. shame/humiliation** (Tomkins, Vol.1, p. 337). Adaptive interactions between infant and caregivers start form the get go, long before language and the kind of reasoning it makes possible, exist. Genetic reconstructions in clinical work are based on inferences regarding the nature of our earliest adaptive responses to interactive experience.

Recognizing natural affect-expressions as a phylogenetically given species-specific signally-system of communication, antedating and independent of language, makes it possible to systematize a hierarchic developmental model of semiotic progressions originating in organic codes, rising through natural signals to learned cultural signs and symbol systems, each associated with *different organizations of experience* and modes of expression. Affect expressions are the behavioral correlates of feelings; they speak directly from and to the human soul. But their spontaneous expression is soon modulated, mediated, and regulated, suppressing unacceptable aspects in a species primed for socio-cultural collaboration, driven to imitate, recognize, organize, signify, and ultimately, symbolize, processed stimuli according to societal norms. Only in regressed states or a non-judgmental "free" space—as in dreams, psychosis, or psychoanalytic dialogues—are feelings again given free reign.

Closing Statements:

Since the mind that isolates natural or cultural signs *qua signs* is also the mind that decodes and interprets their messages, in the interest of systematic study and classification, it is important to honor distinctions between nonlinguistic vs. verbal communicative modes. This is implied in a continuum the logical principles of which must include iconic, oro-gestural, proto-semiotic, as well as signaled or signified forms of communication/ reception, building from this a classificatory system that reflects varieties of *biosemiotic* coded interactions. In this way we actualize B. Russell's (1953) conceptual vision, that "What is feasible is the understanding of general forms" (p. 109). The "scientific philosophy" (p. 109) he envisioned would concern itself with the "analysis and enumeration of logical forms, i.e., with the kinds of propositions that may occur, with the various types of facts" (p. 108). In *Biosemiotics* and *Code Biology,* these relevant facts include all forms of vital inter-action, from molecular codes all the way up to natural signals, cultural signs, and increasingly complex symbol systems, *used* as referential tools. For this is where the line between humans and all other life on earth breaks off: that we devise, adopt, and *make use* of semiotic *instruments* to generate referential meanings that are removed from the senses and thereby become mind.

From Emotional Expression to Signifying Gestures, Vocalized Gestures to Phonemes, Phonemes to Words.

Tullio Rizzini, MD

Il libro che ho il piacere di presentare affronta il problema piu` importante nelle indigini sulla costituzione della lingua, quello della natua dei significati, delle parole.
The book I have the pleasure of presenting confronts the most important problem in the study of the constitution of language, that of the nature of meanings, of words.

—*Prof. R. Ambrosini, introduction to T. Rizzini, 2015*

Dr. Aragno's preceding points on methodology are of extreme relevance to my presentation pertaining to the oral-gestural origins of language: that is, how the "primary process," profoundly embodied in instincts and emotions, transforms and becomes realized through the "secondary process" by means of which the "mind," through the use of the brain, manages to formalize in thought those emotions and sentiments that actually derive from sub-cortical regions. So, language encounters a similar vicissitude: emotions as well as unconscious and preconscious instincts, driven by the limbic system, generate the necessary mimetic gestures for a person to represent themselves to other members of the group enabling that essential inter-species collaboration that is indispensable to survival.

How do we situate human language in this evolutionary context? Though still fashionable, both spiritual and rational theories have given us no valid answers regarding the evidential evolutionary trajectory of language with respect to specifics in the gradual perfecting of informative gestures. And yet a simple reflection is enough to help us understand what the real mechanisms were in establishing language. This reflection consists of comprehending that the oro-facial gestural-mimetic complex, with its specific meanings, preceded and rendered phonetic language possible simply by *phonologizing gestures* while preserving their meanings. It is enough to interpret gestures articulating phonetic sounds, especially those that are consonants, straightforwardly, as gestural pre-phonetic and informative. I have worked for over 30 years in this new approach, interpreting sounds simply as replacing gestures, using ample samples from psychotics who, due to their regressed condition, are closer than others to the collective unconscious. By listening and observing in this way I have been able to infer and establish a contextual-behavioral and ethological *sense* to every phonetic articulation, thereby retracing our species' prelinguistic communication from its visual code.

It seems clear that if articulations that produce phonemes are considered from this new point of view as pre-linguistic informative-gestures, we are obliged to consider their nature as being exquisitely ethological and behavioral, derived, as already mentioned, from subcortical emotional and instinctual innervations. In this way we underscore Dr. Aragno's fundamental concept, that the "primary process" is transformed into the "secondary process" by evolutionary necessity. In fact, we should generalize this Freudian principle, considering it *a veritable evolutionary engine.*

But how then, concretely, did the human species come upon language out of this contextual—behavioral, ethological, informative condition? Obviously, in the most simple, expedient and economical way possible; while preserving the spiritual and emotional sense in these gestures, deriving sounds from them by means of a versatile oral cavity through which air may vibrate in many diverse ways. It is evident that in this way every gesture produces its own phonetic sound not because it *wants* that particular one but because it *can* produce only that one. So, for instance, the sound of P, that we believe we produce voluntarily by imitating our parents, was, instead, realized by our species simply because the compression and swelling of the cheeks could behaviorally express nothing but an extremely useful informative mimetic signal of compression or of power. The sense of the gesture was therefore a threat or an invitation to press and compress.

Likewise, for example, the oral gesture that produced **L** could not but represent information or an invitation to alter or modify something, given that its antecedent, visual gesture was realized through alternatively sticking out the tongue and retracting it. Apparently, the species utilized these pre-linguistic gestures for many centuries, and contemporary linguistics is ever more induced to analyzing the moment in which the real "word" was elaborated.

But on what, then, does the elaboration of words consist when based on this evolutionary conception? The answer is both rational and extremely simple: our species learned to combine the relationship between gestures (and their meanings), much like deaf mute sign-language, and then to combine those sounds derived from gestures, realizing in a second stage, the enormous informative advantage afforded by an acoustic vocabulary. So, to stay with the examples, if **P** means, first of all, pressure, compression, and **L** first of all, alternation, variation, the **PL** ratio has an archetypal meaning such as "variable pressure or variable compression, power," in fact, this meaning is very well suited to the sense of the word Polo or Politics, and many other radical PL words. The rational counterproof of this hypothesis is simply to reverse the bi-consonantal relationship so it will be seen that words with LP partly express, in their historical meaning, a sense of "variation of pressure" as for example in loop, or in lap. Another example: the oro-gesture producing C, highlights the contraction of the muscles of the jaw and for this reason its gestural significance has been statistically interpreted by the psychotic samples as "continuity of effort," a gesture therefore suitable to activate a behavior of contractual defense. The N-producing gesture, similarly, has been interpreted as a sign of brain inclusion, and therefore also of thought, due to its internal para-encephalic vibration. Therefore, the CN report has the archetype meaning "continuity of inclusion, or even thought." In fact, CAN is one of the many object projections of the first meaning, COUNT or KNOW of the second. The evidence of radical reversal is in NC: continuous inclusion, with examples of the NICK type, or Nucleus type.

The logical demonstration, as evinced in my books, is therefore in the great quantity of words that retain in their historical meanings also their archetypal meaning. And recovering that archetypal meaning by an analysis that traces back to those words that have undergone an inversion of their consonants in their roots. The fundamental mechanism exploited by our creators of words was therefore that they had at their disposal a series of archetypal ideas derived from connections between the meanings of articulate-gestures inherited by the species, and being able to project them in an extremely free and creative way onto objects in reality.

This projective mechanism creates the diversity of languages, due to the fact that every nation may gestate and use their own objective projections in relation to their needs and habits. In conclusion, the primitive linguistic code is nothing more than an expressive derivation of the affective-instinctual "primary process" into a gestural and then phonetic "secondary process," finally combined and projected onto real objects. I have carefully examined in 20 languages the presence of the 13 consonant gestures from which 169 basal or archetypal ideas derive. Such ideas should therefore be considered as the basic epistemological categories of linguistic-thought, followed by all the others through the significant interference of other managed sounds. Analytic proof that the 13 consonant gestures, in combinatorial and reversible forms generate word-meanings in the vocabulary of Indo-European languages, may be found in my books.

Lecture VI
With Body in Mind
Embodied Language

... for in the psychical field, the biological field does in fact play the part of the underlying bedrock.

—*S. Freud, 1937, p. 252*

Abstract

Freud founded Psychoanalysis as an experiential method to uncover unconscious processes and phenomena and decode all non-conscious forms of meaning-making. While it was his analytic breakdown of the pictographic dream that gave Freud access to the vocabulary and grammar of the unconscious, it is through a linguistic code that we interpret its meanings.

All knowledge is filtered through and pinned down by some semiotic system; within the limitations and potential of language, we crystallize new concepts through its nominal capacities, by putting things into words. When listening to the unconscious, however, psychoanalysts adopt a highly specialized attentional stance employing all the senses and emotions as instruments of attunement.

This presentation addresses the psychoanalytic interpretive process which, though constrained by language, is not fundamentally linguistic, and will be in two parts: first I will discuss a paradigm suited to the biosemiotic study of all forms of human interaction and communication. Second, I will address some non-linguistic functions to which our cultural code is put: What *is* and what *can* be done with words?

Psychoanalysis is a method created by language: words are our instruments and medium. This positions us optimally to observe different semiotic levels, from organic symptoms and emotional signals, to the sign and symbolic forms of language. Each of these, exposes different levels of organismic organization best systemized in a *developmental continuum* (Aragno, 1997/2016) beginning in pre- and proto-semiotic forms and culminating in symbolic language-use. This multiple-code model reframes theoretical understanding around epigenetic and morphological principles suited to developmental processes bridging biological and psychological organizations.

From this revised and broadened meta-theoretical base, I illustrate how language may express deep unconscious impulses and is made to serve different functions, presenting ten to which speech is put, ending with two that are specific to a dialogue designated the "talking cure."

* * * *

Two years ago, a sceptical biophysicist expressed doubts about the validity of our theory of dreams, based on the fact that he'd had the same exact dream all his life. I responded that it may *appear* to be the same in its manifest content but its "meanings" probably kept changing. We happened to be in the hotel lobby the next day so I invited him to sit down and asked if he would like to tell me the recurring dream; I would sample for him an interpretive session. Welcoming the offer, he believed we were having a simple "conversation." Actually, I was asking pointed questions leading him to talk about his past, his father, his son and other children, his recent retirement and closing of his lab. During those 45 minutes, I reflected back certain key asides and associations he'd made, and by the end offered an interpretation of the deeper more emotionally current meaning of his recurring dream. Not only did he agree, but he was immensely impressed by the seamless, casual way we uncovered its current significance! The point was made that psychoanalysis is an *experiential* process; not *textual* but *contextual,* requiring a vital dialogue and a multi-code, *organismic* model of mind as explanatory base.

Language is a neural code, its specialized functional circuitry is in the brain: in use, however, speech subsumes the whole nervous system fuelled by conscious and unconscious impulses and desires. This talk addresses some extra-linguistic functions observed in analytic sessions to which speech is put and that psychoanalysts interpret.

To begin, however, I would like to say a few words regarding where to place psychoanalysis in the sciences, focusing specifically on its unique role in advancing understanding of the transitional locus where sensory experience becomes mind via the representational processes of dream-imagery. Once recounted and copiously associated to, the dream's deeper meanings are accessible to linguistic interpretation through a transposition from one "form of thought" into another, a translation from one semantic of meanings into another. This sequence, translating a pictorial code into a cultural communicative code—from primary to secondary process cognition—contains a number of valuable insights regarding the layered sources of meaning, imagination, representation, and semiotic progressions. The interpolation of the "sign" in mental organization is fundamentally transforming: Principles of *form and transforming organizations* are the new scientific "laws" for living systems.

At bottom, these are epistemological problems, originating in viewing bodies as matter, mind as air, explained in terms of matter. The legacy of this approach is in seeking *"knowledge"* (as data) rather than *"understanding"*: Consider the distinction made by German philosophers between these two different approaches: *Erklärende*—by way of explanation; and *Verstehende*—by way of understanding.

Changing Paradigms, Paradigms for Change

Mentioned before, here, I provide a more in-depth account of a determining shift. In the thirties and forties, Norbert Weiner (1948) spearheaded a group of scholars from various disciplines studying what McCulloch (1965) called the "Embodiment of mind." At the same time Piaget (1969, 1970), in Switzerland, was researching children's cognitive development; Bateson and Mead in New Guinea were embedded in the naturalistic study of rituals and rites of passage; Maturana and Varela (1980) and others in the Palo Alto group were examining organizations of living forms; and Weiner, a mathematician, was developing *Cybernetics*, a way of discerning *pattern* and *form* as *organization* for a new science of information, one markedly different from physics. Applied to living systems, these could now be studied in terms of interactions, communications, in non-linear recursive patterns of interface in which events have specific *meanings* according to the contextual frames of reference that engender them.

The difference is that of two distinct epistemologies, from the Renaissance until approximately the 1940s, science was founded on deterministic principles based on causes. But causality precludes human elements like purpose, drive, emotion, expression, tone, all based on interactive circumstance and subjective intent. With good reason, Gregory Bateson (1972, 1979), an epistemologist, remarked that Cybernetics was "the biggest bite out of the fruit of the tree of knowledge mankind has taken in the last 2000 years" (1972, p. 476). Arguably, an equally big bite was taken by von Bertalanfy's (1968) Systems Theory. Synthetic thinking evolved in reaction to hard determinism with the idea that a system's functioning must be understood through the *changing organization of its interacting parts internally and in relation to other systems* (Ackoff, 1975). Viewing the organism as essentially active introduced the concept of innate development and wholeness in preserving the "disequilibrium of steady state" (von Bertalanfy, 1968, p. 209): *coherence* occurs spontaneously between interacting systems that come into constant contact. What has impact and what is impacted upon, invoking Heisenberg, will *always* have to be understood as a dialectic, in terms of recursivity. The new scientific "laws" for living systems of *form and transformation* cannot be "quantified" or determined because they are circumstantial and contextual—probabilistic.

Since the mind that isolates natural or cultural signs *qua signs* is also the mind that decodes and interprets their messages, it is important to note that the burden of interpretation rests on the current capacity, purpose, and subjective intent of the interpreter, within a given semantic context. However, in the interest of systematic study, the formal distinctions between nonlinguistic and verbal communicative modes and their reciprocal impact, must be fully taken into account. This is implicit in a continuum the logical principles of which include iconic, emotional, gestural, proto-semiotic, expressive, as well as coded signal and symbolic forms of signification. From this exhaustive array of meaning-modes, a classificatory system may be built that reflects the formal varieties of *biosemiotic* communications in reciprocal interaction. Given that our subject-matter concerns the operative processes of mind itself, in the interest of *scientific* scrutiny, it is important to heed Heisenberg's lesson and be sure to take the mind's *own* functional capacities and current contributions into account, a point that becomes technically imperative in the psychoanalytic "listening stance."

Human interactions are governed from very early on by local linguistic conventions in a predominant semantic orbit that impacts immediately on the young developing mind. Verbal habits, learned early on, contain identifications with caregivers as well as ways in which language was used to manipulate, adapt to, and control, the environment. But language also serves many unconscious embodied demands, and more regressive needs of which the speaker is completely unaware, all of which infiltrate and exploit speech to obtain their goals. These emerge in analysis and our task is to bring them to light. All events in an analysis are *created by speech* by means of a situational protocol in which the analysand "talks freely" while the analyst listens for unconscious meanings. This unevenly embedded situation engenders a regression opening deeper, less differentiated, forms of interaction. For this reason, language takes on many non-linguistic functions while also, conversely, acquiring formidable abstractive levels . . . interests to which I now turn.

The Greek *semeion*—sign, stands for symptom: In *Studies in Hysteria* (Breuer & Freud, 1895), previously inexplicable physical symptoms were found to have unconscious *meaning*s. These emerged gradually and spontaneously as patients were invited to recount and talk freely. Listening to patients in this way, Freud stumbled on the study of a universal product of the deepest unconscious, the dream. Taking it as an object of scienfitic scrutiny, he set about decoding the formal grammar and vocabulary of its pictographc language sprung from personal imagination and unbidden desires. It goes without saying that every dreamer will code meanings in a unique way. Breaking down its meaning-making mechanisms, Freud found the dream's latent *thoughts,* its nodal *ideas,* to be the source-code for the expressive imagery of its manifest content. The definition of "unconscious" widened to encompass both repressed affects, experiences, and thoughts (the etiology of hysterical symptoms) as well as a *normal* underlay of human cogntion and meaning-forms, a scope that requires an epigenetic-developmental semiotic formula to systematize.

But Freud was embedded in a *Weltenschauung* that could not provide appropriate concepts for the theoretical understanding of this transformation from unconscious "presentation" to Pc or Cs *re*presentation, either in image or in verbal form. These *semiotic* shifts from proto-semiotic *presentational* forms to a conventional *re*-presentational *system* as carrier of meanings, may be charted in a revised biosemiotic model of mind (Aragno, 1997/2016).

The aim of science is to identify and systematize operative processes and principles. Yet our "subject-matter"—the human mind—is an intangible concept better described as "organizations of experience" and meaning; the psychoanalyst's task, to uncover its unconscious phenomena and processes. A science dedicated to uncovering the laws of "meaning" along a continuum from unconscious to consciousness requires a scientific bedrock planted in principles of semiotic development. I have been interested in systematizing such principles of biosemiotic progression through a revised developmental model of mind (Aragno, 1997/2016) in relation to a discourse semantic that strives to uncover *all* unconscious phenomena. This multiple-code model accords with phylo- and onto-genetic development, providing hypotheses for micro and macro-genetic psychoanalytic interpretive processes that bridge affects, memory and cognition, soma and psyche, while expanding personal awareness through "working-through" and insight. This model led to an analysis of the *specific* semantic and dialogic features (Aragno, 2008/2016) of a discourse-situation that produces predictable phases and phenomena using neuro-biological mediating processes that modulate affects, increase awareness, and revise personal narratives, generating psychological change.

The paradigm shift underlying the two volumes presenting this model (Aragno, 2016, a & b) brings psychoanalytic meta-theory and clinical practice under one conceptual system of ideas. Through our interpretive processes and dialogical technique, affective/cognitive processes of "working-through" (joining affects and words), slowly produce semiotic transformations yielding deep neurobiological changes that impact mental organization. These events, all created by speech, illuminate what we do and what *can* be done with language, interests to which I now turn.

The Talking Cure Psychoanlysis was born and created by speech—language *in use*. Language is our instrument and medium. Only words are permitted between interlocutors. Yet the situation and its processes are *not* fundamentally linguistic. In fact, the semantic space thereby engendered generates one of the most intimate and incendiary of all human sitautions!! How is this so? It is because our interpretive agenda opens levels of inter-action that sink below the bounded conventions of individual-separateness and linguistic exchange. Here, the body speaks—emotions are set loose, and memory emerges in reenactments. The semantic of the unconscious is multilevelled, polysemic—including signals, signs, and symbolic modes—its deep expressions crossreference all senses confusing present with past, resurfacing old emotion in new experience, many of its meanings organized at embodied, pictured, enactive and transmissive levels, involving the whole organism. The unconscious speaks in multi-coded ways issuing *directly* from the body in overtly somatic as well as in highly attuned and metaphoric forms. Dream imagery is the body's boldest and most direct expression of what is pressing on the mind and how one feels about it.

Since our task is to meet comunications at the communicants' current level, we are required to engage the whole sensorium in our listening stance, to reach *into* and become attuned to what is not uttered but enacted, not remembered but shown, not said but transmitted, projected, implied, and often, denied. The body enters language through many different unconscious pathways creating a semantic zone, or orbit, of non-verbal sensibilities; it enters the situation, the interactions, the process and its fluid inter-penetrative communicative layers, reaching below the limen of consciousness via somatizations, actions, expressive tone, gesture, emotional outbursts, and dreams—*most directly* in dreams where the body is memory, artist, spinner of desire, and metaphorizing problem-solver, all in one. The dream depicts felt-ideas *as images*. And it does so acquainting us over time with the dreamer's unique vocabulary of categories, stereotypes, prototypes, beliefs, fears, and patterns of self-fulfilling prophecies.

The psychoanalytic principle of regression, as in psychosis and dreams, is well served by a model of mind that proposes an epigenetic continuum from the earliest undifferentiated sensorimotor synesthesia at birth, through layers of semiotic infiltration via gestures and language, to the higher abstractions of mediated thought. Our earliest experiences are unrepresented, encoded directly in *the body*. These schemata are laid down as patterns of inter-action—soothing or frustrating, embracing or abrasive, safe or unsettling—creating an experiential template toward which later experiences orient. What anything *means* is, and *remains, first* related to how it *feels*. This sensori-emotive matrix will be heavily overlaid by mediations, socializing expressions, actions and gestures accompanied by words, and gradually by the conventionalizing modulations of language. But the raw sensorimotor core—the true Self—remains, its formidable imprint and authentic intelligence returning unfettered in the private composite imagery of dreams.

The body emerges via a few key unconscious channels that are of particular interest to psychoanalysis: the most direct is *somatization*, or "organ language," of which we observe two kinds: symptoms without any physical cause, as in hysterical disorders, and symptoms where unconscious determinants are contributing to the disease's severity. The body also seeps into free-associative speech through expressive channels that qualify hidden meanings i.e., speed of recounting, facial and gestural expressions, movements, tone, volume, and the constant subliminal undercurrent of metaphorical allusions, all point to implicit meanings. And finally, the body imposes itself on language, making it serve many non-linguistic functions that substitute for emotional and relational needs.

Listening to the unconscious requires constant self-vigilant *empathy* and a cross-referencing of stimuli coming from multiple levels and forms of communication simultaneously. Psychoanalysts treat speech as *significant behavior*, noting how communication affects sensibilities that must be attuned to feelings and meanings normally out of reach. Interrelationships between form and content are all important here since unconscious meanings wedge between tone, action, and word.

Ten Speech Functions

Identifying the following ten speech-functions that mix and overlap is helpful when viewing speech as an organismic activity serving many extra-linguistic dynamic purposes and functions.

1. The first is maintaining ***contact***: here, the vocal line is a thread, an umbilical cord or psychic cell-phone, serving to make and sustain a constant connection. Of course, there are degrees of intensity with which attachment is pursued depending on whether it is motivated by separation-anxiety, a need for attention, social interaction, emotional connectedness, or intellectual exchange. Regardless, the desired response implies a reciprocal investment in the interaction.

2. The second is ***discharge***: here, the vocal stream serves as an exhaust-valve to release various types of physiological, emotional, or psychological

tensions. Words are used to eject, project, ventilate, and eliminate, undesirable tensions, sensations, or unmanageable mental states. Used as weapons, they become instruments of rage. Early analysts noted that words become substitutes for bodily substances (Sharpe, 1940): patients use speech to discharge oral, anal, and phallic drives, to masturbate, obtain exhibitionistic and narcissistic satisfaction, and may endow the analyst's speech with identical or complementary meanings (Rycroft, 1958, p. 413). When speech serves such quasi-organic purposes, analysts are called on to perform container functions; from garbage pail to gilded mirror, toilet bowl to cherished vessel, from impartial listener to soothing, comforting organizer and holder.

3. The third is ***thought***: originating in the egocentric "inner-speech" of childhood, this vibrant monologic verbal commentary gradually turns inward, persisting as the stream of consciousness that accompanies our experiences and steers our actions. It is this same stream, we try to tap and set free, re-externalized in free associations, to "observe" another's mind. The use of language in *concentrated* thought, however, is more deliberate and focused, as in planning, reasoning, deciding, reconstructing a memory, strategizing, or, most particularly, in the "abstraction" of ideas.

4. The fourth is ***play***: here, words are toys and, speech itself, an instrument of hilarity. From baby's babble and childhood word-games, to puzzles, punning, rhyming, joking, parodying, and verbal sparring, people love to have fun with language. Teasing, flirtation, humor, and humoring, are all done with words as indispensable accoutrements of interactions that seem to rise out of and flower through speech, so that language and laughter—a highly infectious pair—intermingle and are often tied together.

5. The fifth is the ***informative*** function of speech: and, were it not for our pervasive search for unconscious meanings, it might be as straightforward as it appears—a means for imparting information. But no piece of information, however simple, is devoid of surrounding qualifiers and contextual implications—the reasons for it coming up now; what came before, and what follows; what is being done simultaneously, *how* it is communicated, its metaphorical implications, transferential shadings, etc., so that a psychoanalytic inquiry is incomplete without attempting to grasp a whole array of possible meanings... and, a cigar is rarely, if *ever*, just a cigar!

6. The sixth is ***metabolizing*** (as in working-through): here speech is processing intensely charged intense experiences, emotions, and memories. The purpose is to express, organize, narratize, and slowly *neutralize* traumatic memories and feelings. Revisiting and giving meaning to subjectively tainted memories, constructs new, more complete narratives. Words are instrumental in formulating, describing, depicting, articulating, sharing, and modulating qualities of profoundly stirring or disturbing experiences, thereby defusing their physiological hold through the transformative action of verbalization. The metabolizing function of "telling," or being witnessed, also subsumes the contact, discharge, expressive, integrative and transformative functions of speech.

7. The seventh is ***conceptualizing***; here speech serves the strictly symbolic and cognitive/intellectual functions of formulating, articulating, elaborating, abstracting, and deliberating on *ideas*. As an extension or continuation of thought, conceptualizing is the concentrated gestation and manipulation of ideas at high levels of abstraction. When listening to this kind of speech we are, similarly, induced to "think about," invited into the articulation of ideas.

8. The eighth function I have called ***aesthetic*** or ***poetic***, because it is the most expressive, inspired, evocative, and deeply personal articulation of speech. It springs from imaginative creative sources and artistic sensibilities that impel the speaker to craft words that generate a novel, aesthetic envisagement. This kind of lyrical speech, given to those who have "a way with words" touches us, engendering a *participatory* response insofar as we are able to enter-into its suggestive evocations.

9 &10. The ninth and tenth, ***integrative*** and ***transformative*** functions of speech are specific to key processes of our clinical "method," and reflect the full "linking'" scope and semiotic capacities of "working-through" afforded by "putting things into words" in speech. This applies specifically to personal insight obtained within psychoanalytic contexts and is achieved through its therapeutic action and intent, consisting of identifying, naming, and bringing into the dialogic linguistic orbit that which was enacted and/ or "unsayable," before.

The *integrative* function joins differently organized experiences, i.e., linking affects with words, image with meaning, past with present, psychic-reality with secondary processing thought. In the *transformative* function, the analyst's words are catalytic, aiming to effectuate a complete transmutation in the nature of how experiences are now narratized and known, accompanied by a transposition in the *form* through which they are communicated. The *integrative* function brings together, unifies, and consolidates the personality: through linguistic articulation, when uttered personally; *transformative* speech indicates that working-through and profound psychological change is in progress.

The two functions work synergistically, the former paves the way, making possible the high degree of self-awareness and higher levels of synthetic and symbolic organization expressed through the latter. Both functions imply the activity of a steadily working new reflexive referential structure, the "observing ego" which, in turn, is developed as part of the requisite cognitive equipment of the "analytic attitude." The analyst's stance, style of inquiry and, particularly, theoretical penchant, simultaneously model the means and steer the referential perspectives, for self-reflection while utilizing language as a symbolic tool for deep psychological understanding.

Insight gained in psycho-analytic interactions is integrative because it comes about through lived experience in contextual repetitions that render palpable how past shadings are contaminating current colors, clouding the ability to see and cope with current reality. The analyst's sensibilities and skill in moving between barely preconscious apperceptions and their symbolic organization in thought and language is technically requisite so that higher organization of material, hitherto inaccessible and less organized, may be communicated verbally to the analysand. The psycho-cognitive instrumentation of the psychoanalytic semantic is implemented through the dialectics of its discourse processes and interpretive use of verbal form.

In summary: language names things and represents experience, so it matters which experiences are named and how they are represented in the pursuit of conscious awareness. "Words," in other words, make us conscious as they give us the means to connect with others...

To be continued...

Lecture VII
Embodied Dialogue
Words as Deeds in Psychoanalytic Semantic Fields

The life of mind is a totality of levels, which on one hand exist side by side, but which on the other, appear transitorily one after the other. The moments which the mind seems to have left behind actually exist in it at the present time in full depth.
—Hegel, Lectures on Philosophy of History (1807), Sämmtliche Werke, 9.

Abstract

This presentation addresses the interpretive implications of referencing multi-code meanings in the framework of a revised biosemiotic, developmental model of mind and communication (Aragno, 1997/2016, 2008/2016). Freud's "scientific method" is an interpretive dialogue tailored to give maximum access to uncovering unconscious processes and meanings. As a method designed specifically for this purpose, its tilted, unconventional, interlocutory protocol and interpretive agendas establish a complex multileveled, biosemiotic semantic field triggering many regressive processes that reveal pre- and non-linguistic communicative forms. The required listening/observational stance also exposes embodied unconscious expressions that have little to do with surface linguistic content, to which these relate only metaphorically.

In this bi-directional orchestration of multi-coded (body/mind) complexity, wherein the sole interpretive instrument permitted is language, word-meanings may partially dissolve their semiotic structuring, expressing underlying emotional needs and more primitive embodied drive origins.

The renowned tree-of-life image is a metaphor, model, and research tool, used to explore the evolution of life and to describe relationships between living organisms, as in a famous passage of Charles Darwin's *On the Origin of Species* (1895). Its universal appeal, however, may be generalized to serve other epigenetic, multi-level conceptualizations. I will make ample use of this natural iconic template to illustrate major underlying themes of my talk.

* * * *

This represents a transition for me. I will revisit and clarify some things from my talk two years ago, and indicate where I intend to go from here. As a psychoanalytic meta-theoretical revisionist, my area of expertise is psychoanalysis. In both its experiential practice and complex polysemic scientific base, psychoanalysis is a difficult, often devalued, method; at best misunderstood, at worst, misjudged. Freud anticipated this, realizing that his descriptive metaphors for his observations were not adequate for the phenomena he was bringing too light. Those who followed would have to advance the meta-theory for psychoanalysis to be accepted into scientific communities. This, I have striven to do. But from now on, psychoanalysis will become a springboard to enter into a vast new area of research within the Barbierian, Code Biology, theoretical framework. My question then becomes how psychoanalytic knowledge may contribute to a line of inquiry that follows logically from a revision of Freud's first theory of mind and, further, what can our method and canon *already* say about the topics I approach?

A developmental psychology of the unconscious with a broad purview of inquiry demands inter-disciplinary scholarship for its advancement. Its method, however, is simply a dialogue: we use language as an instrument of interpretation and psychological insight. Our inquiry, therefore, enters the human mind top-down; molecular biologists come to it, bottom up. Nevertheless, to study *all* coding processes we must address the human organism, whole; cells, nervous system, brain, the seat of mind, other uniquely human executive functions, language, and the codes of culture that are learned. Whereas Freud began with a failed attempt at a neurologically based project for a scientific psychology (1895), he later stayed away from neuroanatomical correlates. Today we cannot ignore a century of neuroscientific advances, especially since they undergird the neurobiological processes leading to conscious awareness of the analytic process. For Freud, the organic/biological underlay *was* the true unconscious: "The physiological substrate does not end once the psychical begins but rather creates a psycho-physical parallelism a 'dependent concomitant.'" (1915, p. 207) This implies a multilayered, body/mind affair. For this reason, my revisions emphasize epigenesis and continuity with the body. A sensori-motor core remains throughout life, and the body's expressions continue to seep through words and acts regardless of semiotic level or medium used. Nowhere is this continuity between biological and psychical more clearly expressed than in dreams which, straddling both, form a link from one to the other.

My talk on embodied language was designed to illustrate, through twelve examples, what our multi-level, psychoanalytic listening stance can yield in tapping unconscious motivation and sense. While free associations flow along a surface linguistic line, what is being *done* and elicited through speech, that is, *unconscious meanings and intent,* stem from deeper drives and emotional needs. In a hierarchic web of communicative modes, the higher cultural system masks a non-verbally coded underlay of primitive impulsions. At the end of my talk, I was criticized: "this was all about psychoanalysis but said nothing about code biology." At first, I was stunned. I thought that what I presented had everything to do with illustrating multiple layers of diversely-coded human communication. But then, reconsidering the criticism, here is what I learned; what seemed obvious and implicit to me may not be so for listeners from other fields; a term I use metaphorically, assuming its meaning, as in "channels of communication," may be heard concretely by those dealing with aluminum pipes or neuronal axes: the immense amount of condensed knowledge pressed into the words "psyche or mind" for me, may be ephemeral and illusory to someone who studies cells, neurons, and dendrites. In other words, language matters, nowhere more than in interdisciplinary contexts like this one.

We may all converge generally on the topic of codes but we each come to it from different angles, using terms from different linguistic spheres— conceptually and practically. The semantic here, broadly defined, is still diffuse and needs to develop a joint vocabulary with each participant spelling out their definitions and goals, not assuming everyone understands what they are talking about. Freud's discoveries opened up a new semantic sphere in human awareness: that of an omnipresent unconscious. This is how consciousness of *anything* occurs—through specific linguistic articulation *in* dialogue. The psychoanalytic subversive focus on the unconscious led to detecting meaning in hysterical symptoms, decoding the dream's pictographic vocabulary, uncovering the latent significance of the manifest sign. Additionally, psychoanalytic dialogues create unique ***semantic fields*** due to their mandate, to investigate all things unconscious. And this has relevance here; all group-dialogues create semantic fields. The importance of context (deixis), its conceptual "frame," purpose, and protocol in dialogues, discussions, and conferences, cannot be overemphasized. Context determines the meaning of words and terms used in the semantic domain of inquiry, a sphere whose orbits will expand and spread, generating new conscious awareness.

This leads me to my first use of the tree template: molecular/evolutionary biologists are represented in the seeds and cellular roots of a tree whose trunk, codex (caudex) in Latin, 'Code,' is our central conceptual pillar. Out of this "codex/trunk" grow other semiotic branches, representing other disciplines, here yielding leaves, flowers, and the fruits of interdisciplinary discourse and conceptual cross-fertilization. There can be no flowers or fruits without branches, no branches without a trunk, no trunk without roots and seeds. Whether the word 'code' is used or not, the omnipresence of this core conceptual *fulcrum* ought to be implicit.

* * * *

I turn now to methodology: the Code Biology charter calls for the study of all codes of life by the standard methods of science. But let us be clear; psychoanalysis deals with "mind," the "unconscious," "psyche," the Greek word for soul, all abstract concepts for "phenomena" that cannot be *seen,* descriptives for ideas about what goes on "inside" their functional seat— the brain. So, in psychoanalysis we study mental phenomena through their *manifestations* in a research method designed to make whatever is unconscious conscious; personal meanings in therapy, general principles in a meta-theory of mind. Established just over a hundred years ago, Freud's first model—Ucs, Pcs, Cs,—was effective descriptively but had no explanatory power: it could not explain the transformation from unconscious to conscious awareness through talking, and was couched metaphorically in homeostatic and Newtonian principles. Today, updated, revised, and supplemented by a century of advances in the neurosciences and early development, we have a better idea of how to map an explanatory model of conscious awareness based on plausible semiotic operative principles.

The "mind" does one thing: it re-presents experience; the semiotic process is its medium. Reinforced and dramatically reorganized by language; this process follows a developmental sequence contingent on a multitude of vicissitudes from inside and outside. Through this singular capacity, our minds accomplish all the brilliant diverse feats of imagination, invention, calculation and creation, that we associate with our species! Human brains are pattern-makers: we are pattern-finders, pattern re-creators and repeaters; this is how we organize stimuli, learn, habituate, and crystallize experience into memory. Innate signifying processes organizing human experience begin at birth in the perceptual gestalt, sensori-motor schemas, and a "primary process" form of cognition that is soon overlaid by a "secondary process" governed by language that modulates behavior by mediating communication as it socializes. Language introduces linearity (through syntax), time, convention, the "and-then" of narration and causality, all absent from the "primary-process mode," a compositional semantic that reappears in art and dreams.

So, psychoanalysts are comfortable with inference, metaphor, metonymy, analogy, enactment, and especially with *pattern detection.* We are interested in subtle inter-active dynamics, in grasping a repetitive pattern leading into subjective experience and its origins; less interested in conscious talking than picking up the metaphorical message implied, expressing unconscious meanings transmitted through different channels, like a radio picking up particular frequencies. Body, mind, and communication, are not separate in a semantic of unconscious meanings that exhibits the interwoven nature of all three. Language is itself embedded in sensory-affective experience emanating from bodily strata that, like a basso continuo, provide perpetual undertones of latent meanings to higher-clef surface content. Human mental life is multilayered, polysemic; multi-coded sign-processes operate simultaneously all the time.

Psychoanalytic development research, especially into early mirroring and attachment phenomena, has much to say that complements cognitive neuroscience thanks to our dialectical *in vivo* approach. We look into mind *with* mind; a science that bends back to observe its own constructs. And this points to my role here—I come to biological underpinnings top-down, from a cultural code *into* organic semantic spheres. So, although I may begin to veer away from strictly psychoanalytic premises, I will not abandon the monumental corpus of advancements in knowledge from our literature of over a century that must be integrated to broach new interdisciplinary challenges.

For now, let me turn to our tree again, this time to illustrate the developmental model of symbolization and communication (Aragno, 1997/2008/2016) from which I have operated thus far, transposed from its diagram on the page. This is an explanatory model for how dialogue generates conscious awareness, how we become aware of *being aware* through specific talking. I should add that the great Soviet team of Vygotsky and Luria (1963), studying concept-awareness and language-use in the rural Ural Mountains, emphasized that we become conscious *specifically* of some-*thing*; awareness is not an objectified abstraction but, rather, is tied to specific word-sense in a particular *dialogic semantic* and social context. This is extremely important in my view.

The roots of our Tree now represent phylogenetic givens, present at birth, namely eight primary emotional expressions, instinctual rooting, sucking, the visual cliff, and perceptual patterning (a coding instinct?). The trunk we may view as the body's first sensori-motor stage leading from single words and brief phrases into language proper. Here, at the juncture where branches begin to sprout, is also the "dream" appearing as portal and bridge between the organic un-representable into re-presented pictographic form. Other branches with leaves may be viewed as the multitude of functions to which language is put, and the great leap in semiotic advancement it promotes in cognition and learning. Among these are recounting, story-telling, reading, writing, reflection, abstraction, dialogue, debate. Higher branches represent other semiotic systems (mathematics, music-notation, etc.) and diverse discourse-semantics, the topmost branches reaching the high abstractions of reflexive, poetic, and conceptual thought.

Stratified layering is expressed in an epigenetic continuum of six stages of semiotic mediation organized hierarchically, moving from natural signals, through acquired signs, to symbolic organization. This model moves from primal, natural signals, through proto-semiotic gestural/verbal signs, to linguistic and dialogic semiotic progressions, creating a multilayered framework composed of plains of *mental organization* that corresponds to cerebral architecture. These levels of organization are fluid, each superseded by the next, but none disappear completely and remain subject to return in regression. The functional continuity of this organismic model (Aragno, 1997/2008/2016) provides a unifying framework that presumes the biological origins of cognition, subsuming proto-semiotic modes and their gradual mediation through semiotic development. Implicit is the integration of emotion with cognition, the organic with the symbolic, a unity that assigns to the whole nervous system the center of the organism's regulatory controls. The heuristic value of the dream's many condensed, coded, signifying mechanisms is theoretically enhanced as most of these are precursors to linguistic tropes: metaphor, metonymy, synecdoche, analogy, all first appear in iconic form. The implications of this model, however, are broader, making psychoanalysis an epistemology (a way of knowing) within a special discourse-semantic framework.

This is a rough, highly abbreviated overview of my developmental model of symbolization (Aragno,1997/2016) designed to update, expand, and transpose into semiotic processes Freud's three systems of mind, Ucs, Pcs Cs, separated "spatially" in a mental topography of states of consciousness, each incomprehensible to the others.

In addition to *repression* and *regression*, two pillars of psychoanalytic theory, here are some key premises underlying this revised model of mind and communication:

1. Epigenesis and morphology as *developmental principles* generating layered plains of mental organization governed by *morphological* changes in semiotic forms; shifts in *functional-form* thereby determine discrete mental organizations, a concept corresponding to the "configurational properties of the underlying neural circuitry" (R. Sperry, personal communication in Gazzaniga, 2018, p. 229).

2. A general movement from simple *signal-sign* forms to increased complexity in the densely compressed abstraction of higher *symbolic* form.

3. Beginning in an undifferentiated state, mental development evolves, assisted by semiotic steps, through obligatory intra-psychic stages of increasing self-object differentiation.

4. A crucial interrelatedness between form, content, and context, in considering and understanding meaning and sense.

5. Discourse and dialogue generate *semantic fields* of *specific* awareness. Only *explicit* verbalization of *being aware* indicates full conscious-cognizance.

This revision of Freud's first model of mind (the topographical) correlates with neurobiological processes. More importantly it is a model of semiotic development that fits the Barbierian framework for which reason I migrated from a group that adheres to a categorially-mistaken definition of semiosis for organic cells with which I could not concur. The Peircean analysis of semiosis pays insufficient attention to its origins, evolution, and development, ontogenetically and phylogenetically. It is an objectified definition of semiosis, telling us little about embodied or changing signifying *processes* to be theoretically complete.

A discourse-semantic where the interpretive slant is toward everything unconscious produces a semantic field wherein less differentiated channels of communication are reopened. Where a controlled formal regression generates a partial breakdown of subject/subject separateness, the analyst must complement the analysand's state creating a communicative field of potentially explosive interpersonal consequence, hence, the advocated opaqueness and neutrality of the analytic stance. Most sciences use instruments to see, hear, probe, picture, record; we alone are the instruments of a *methodology* that is both science and interpretive art. Our method asks that the human mind uncover itself through the dialectic of a specialized dialogue: a science in which we look into ourselves objectively while observing and feeling our Subjects, as topics of inquiry. A participant/observer position where the instrument is *identical* to its subject, paradoxically, requires intense objective-attunement! Our technical stance (Freud's own) is sensitized to bodily signals, signs, and enacted patterns, receptive to metaphors and unconscious messages while remaining vigilant observers of interpersonal dynamics, anchoring our investigation in biological roots. This attentional disposition engages the whole organism's attunement to multi-coded layers of a full spectrum of meaning-forms, including less differentiated unmediated ones appearing as symptoms, transmitted, projected, or reenacted, and viewing these *as data*. Ours is a polysemic science which, like anthropology, uses manifest clues to uncover the archeology of the epigenetic principles of mind.

The receptive analyst is attuned to transmissive frequencies through a heightened resonance to inductions that simultaneously replay whole interactive dynamisms (context, object, feelings) *directly shown* via projective enacted means. The task is to detect this hybrid input. Not only is the listener part of the field of observation, but *the way* the observer observes, quantum-like, is *crucial* to what is detected. The yields of this method are contingent on the attunement, knowledge, and interpretive sensibilities of the observing/listener as they *also* reveal how memory, meanings, and motives operate. This is what is meant by "embodied" dialogue; that the *human biological sensori-emotive underbelly participates cognitively in the linguistic interpretive field,* illustrating the integrative effect of bringing unconscious expression to conscious verbal exchange.

Words in our dialogues are acts. We do things with words that are done nowhere else, using them insistently, persistently, to identify and refer to what is coded unconsciously. Psychoanalytic contexts are bi-directional semantic fields that expand the mundane functions of linguistic referents to include wordless induction, evocation, and indicative enactments that *themselves* become *forms of reference:* Where nonverbal communications are indices of meaning, words *are deeds*—organic and symbolic. Across the current spectrum of neuro-cognitive and linguistic studies the notion of 'embodied' language, dialogue, even embodied abstract ideation (Gallese, 2018), is at the cutting edge of modern brain/mind research. For those familiar with Freud's theories and Piaget's genetic epistemology, both of which place cognitive beginnings *in the body,* this is not news. Everything 'mental' emanates from a sensori-motor-emotive core.

Remaining questions are many: What occurs *before* the neural clustering of "dynamic schematization"? What came before the metaphoric structuring and primary-process signifying mechanisms of the dream-codes? How did the brain evolve to use this coagulant process to regroup stimuli, what are its manifest products? Is there, or can we even assign "meaning" to organic codes? What is the source-point, the fountainhead, of representation? Is there a primordial cerebral neural code that set this exclusively human capacity in motion, as Barbieri (2006, 2011), Calvin (1996, 1998), Deheane (2014) and others propose? If so, what can it be likened to? Clearly, these are areas where interdisciplinary efforts might go.

* * * *

So far, I have followed Freud's vision by bringing forward a revised neurobiological approach to the study of mind presenting the yields of our method in terms of their theoretical import. My inquiries have focused on the central importance of *semiotic processes and systems* on human mental functioning, a study that is incomplete without an evolutionary trajectory shadowing the ontogenetic developmental line. Now, it seems, that in order to move forward I must telescope back in time taking a more *bio-neurological* approach. And in this too, Freud predicted that peering through and beneath the "dream" psychoanalytic methodology could play an important scientific role.

To be continued . . .

Intermezzo

At the end of this presentation there were questions and comments, some bewildering, showing how far many participants were from understanding the points I was making or even the meaning of some of the words used. However, the head-on criticism from Professor Barbieri who, up until then had been a staunch supporter, was hard to take. He complained that this was all about psychoanalysis but said nothing about Code Biology. I tried to explain that it addressed the embodied nature of language through an interpretive slant that picked up many kinds and levels of coded meanings, enacted, projected, implied, etc., through many unconscious channels of communication. But he remained unconvinced.

An argument ensued in which I ended up in tears. Though not couched as productive criticism, I could *try to use* it productively. In a way it was true; I had been leaning on psychoanalytic material and knowledge, avoiding pushing myself into new territory. A prominent member of our New York psychoanalytic community and a reader of one of my papers had said, "this begs for more" urging me to go further back, before the Freudian primary process. What, I asked myself, was I avoiding, and where ought I now venture; through the "dream" and into prehistory? Paramount to me were honoring Freud's opus and vision and a staunch commitment to the traditions of our interdisciplinary methodology.

And then the Coronavirus hit! The world stopped.

Everything was cancelled, and global lockdown became a perfect opportunity to buckle down and study. The path opened spontaneously as it lay semi-cleared before me through what I had already been working on: in order to go forward, I realized, I *had* to go backward in time. So, after almost 40 years in the psychoanalytic literature, I looked ahead, gave thanks for Amazon, and ordered books! This entrance into an evolutionary dimension necessitated many areas of new readings in the cognitive- and evolutionary-neurosciences, the emotions, comparative psychology, paleo-anthropology, and psycho-history, culling ideas from Biosemiotics, more basically organized by the entire Barbierian theoretical framework. I found myself in a vast interdisciplinary jungle needing, once again, to select kernels of the most pertinent data to synthesize and try to move my understanding forward. What struck me most as I waded through these readings was the usual problem of overspecialization: looking through the lens of one field necessarily misses crucial points made by another. But most bewildering of all was that despite the new *embodied* neuroscientific evolutionary-developmental (evo-devo) approach to mind integrating feelings, DREAMS, were not taken as the entry point for an evolutionary perspective. Yet, as Freud foretold, and I believe, dreams are the very observational *portal and inroad* to the biological entry-point to mind, possibly the *evolutionary juncture*, as body becomes mind!

Embarking on this new inquiry, I questioned what was uniquely psychoanalytic that could contribute to a contemporary interdisciplinary discussion of the natural history of semiosis. The question formed into: How did we become the only species capable of using "re-presentation" and therefore of evolving *semiosis* as an instrument of mind? Finding this continuity in correlation with Freud's theory of Dreams is assisted by Barbieri's code-based model of organic semiosis, and his finding deep parallels between the origins of life and the origins of mind. Barbieri's basic functional template—copy and code—has strong appeal and wide applicability. What was of overarching value was the supraordinate paradigm of biological continuity he proposed.

In a nutshell, Barbieri's (2011) model stands on the premise that genuine novelties are brought about when two domains are brought together by a bridging system based on adaptors (codemakers): the parallel he draws is between processes that generate proteins and those generating feelings (p. 380) in the sense that feelings are brain *artifacts* generated by a code-maker, according to the rules of a *neural code*, "... the brain produces the mind by assembling neural components together with the rules of a neural code, very much as the cell produces proteins with the rules of the genetic code (Barbieri, 2006, p. 382). According to this model, the code-maker in question is the intermediate brain (the system formed by all the intermediate neurons that provide a bridge between sensory and motor neurons). In view of this, the parallels between this paradigm and the processes of assemblage in dynamic-schematization leading to metaphoric processes of dreams, are quite striking, metaphor being the bridge between bodily unrepresented experience and the mind's first re-presented "felt-idea." Moreover, the "copy and code" template is quite evident in the propensity to evoke a visual image to express non-literal *meanings*, thereby "coding" an *idea* that cannot yet be expressed otherwise.

From the lockdown on, my new mission became tracing the origins and natural history of human semiotic functions, persistently exploring how, and in what ways, the Freudian theory of dreams and method of interpretation could fill the gap in this evolutionary trajectory. The three major macro-evolutionary stages in Barbieri's framework provided a perfect avenue to explore all manifest-products and expressions of our unique semiotic capacities, yielding, after Lecture VII, the subsequent series of interconnected lectures.

Lecture VIII
Paradigm for the Living
Evolutionary/Developmental Principles of Process and Inter-action

Let us examine not how observation, facts and data, are built up into general systems of physical explanation, but how these systems are built into our observations, and our appreciation of facts and data.

—*N.R Hanson, 1958, p. 3*

Our consciousness of the perceived world yields us an objective system, which is a fusion of mere data and modes of thought about those data.

—*Whitehead, 1927, p. 37.*

What is feasible is the understanding of general forms.

—*B. Russell 1953, p. 109*

Abstract

This presentation lays the foundations for a shift: from a fundamentally psychoanalytic-based body of knowledge to a wider evolutionary/ developmental approach to the natural history of *signification*. Applying this new poly-disciplinary perspective and to affect a radical conceptual shift, I have had to vastly expand my frame of reference superimposing new areas of research and information on all previous knowledge; in essence, create a synthesis.

The Coronavirus lockdown of 2020 provided an enforced opportunity to think and tackle new areas of study. It made clear that to go forward I had to go backward in time. Adding to years of interdisciplinary readings, I armed myself with recent literature in cognitive- and evolutionary-neuroscience, comparative developmental psychology, the emotions, paleo-anthropology, and psycho-history. Going forward, I will apply this new body of knowledge to Barbieri's basic tenets within his broad three-phased macro-evolutionary design of Organic, Neural, and Cultural forms of semiosis.

I ask what a psychoanalytically informed approach may adduce from contemporary research on the evolution of the human brain/mind in terms of the natural development of semiosis. Via conceptual reconstruction and inference, this poses the question: How did our singular species begin using "re-presentation," devising carriers of signification as instruments of mind? To approach this and related topics methodically, I needed to lay out a set of core principles for a new paradigm, which I herewith present.

This, and presentations going forward, form an interconnected series. Here, I lay out a detailed list of core principles guiding a developmental/ evolutionary approach to semiosis that underlies my examination of select topics within Barbieri's three macro-evolutionary stages.

* * * *

Human psychology is tied to the human nervous system and brain. As a psychoanalyst, therefore, my competence starts at the neural level in Barbieri's framework. But in order to find threads of continuity from coding processes at the start of life through evolutionary development to higher more complex levels of semiosis, I needed to re-orient my thinking, to find an episteme *for how to* approach integrating a new body of data from this broader perspective.

Freud (1900) believed that the dream's unconscious meaning-forms reveal "a picture of our phylogenetic childhood—a picture of the development of the human race of which the individual's development is . . . an abbreviated recapitulation influenced by the chance circumstance of life" (p. 549). With advances in neuroscience and developmental research, and using this window to reconstruct certain evolutionary/developmental semiotic processes, it may now be possible to trace this course. Once again, I mention Freud, Piaget, Barbieri's opus, and E.O. Wilson's consilience call to unify the sciences and humanities, because their transdisciplinary approach undergirds my study of the natural history of semiosis.

A perspective that takes manifest signs ranging from organic symptoms to symbolic abstractions as signifying latent meanings is *a priori* adopting a semiotic lens. Across pre- and chronicled history, we have many manifest signs in skeletal remains, tools, engravings, cave art, early objects, sites of worship and burial grounds, suggesting ways of life and systems of belief that provide insights into early cognition. All point to the evolutionary effects of hominid activities on brain-growth and particularly on the reciprocal impact of the socio-cultural and interpersonal on the explosive use of signs and symbolic representation in the development of mind.

Addressing signifying processes at the neural juncture between body and mind and translating the dream's *"primary process"* pictographic-cognition into *"secondary process"* linguistic-cognition, psychoanalysis reveals how conventional words narrow our frame of reference, concealing many vastly more subtle human impressions, emotions, and meanings. But how organic/cerebral processes build towards this coagulate of dynamic-schemas erupting in dream-imagery is yet to be charted, and neuroscience does not connect brain-imaging specifically to this, our universal and *only* manifest peek into how unconscious "felt-cognition" becomes mind.

What may a psychoanalytically informed approach adduce from contemporary research on the evolution of the human brain/mind regarding the natural development of semiosis? Could Barbieri's "copy and code" formula beginning at microbiological levels be reiterated at higher more complex organizations of the nervous system, manifesting in different ways? How and in what ways did our singular species begin using "re-presentation," ultimately devising carriers of signification as instruments of mind?

The human *semiotic-function* is a mental instrument originating in the sensing body that enables humans to "hold in mind" what is not present to the senses. It is our instrument of thought and communication. Implemented interpersonally, this begins early. Semiosis impacts the *whole* organism engaging the brain/mind in multiple ways in neural loops involving all body-systems, producing interconnections, augmentations, and elaborations, of many cerebral regions and functions, especially once language is acquired. This function enables us to imagine, communicate, crystalize ideas, remember, ponder problems, pose questions, imagine, make plans, assign and create meanings, expressed through multiple media. While semiosis may have originated in re-cognition, in simple acts of imitation, labeling, and encoding, its cerebral underpinnings exploited these seeds over millennia and evolved, layer upon layer, to generate the archeological architecture of our modern human mind. The "triune" brain (MacLean, 1973) formula depicts an evolutionary progression from a core "reptilian" brainstem preserving autonomic vital functions, over which superimpose a limbic system, housing mnemonic and emotional circuits that are heavily interconnected through a thalamic causeway reaching the cortical mantle, an area that is open to new learning. Whereas we share some anatomical similarities with other species, thanks to our densely packed, convoluted cortex, we depart *radically* when it comes to our instrumentation of signs and symbols to generate and elaborate *ideas*.

Going forward I will be building on Barbieri's foundational microbiological work on the origins of life and superimpose on this an inquiry into our species' development of semiosis, seeking a continuous thread from molecular processes to the highest forms of cognitive abstraction; to identify how this template reiterates up a hierarchy at various levels of organization. To do this requires a phylo- and onto-genetic approach. Knowing nothing about molecular biology I take experts at their word in seeking continuity from coding processes at the start of life through their long evolutionary progression in the human nervous system and into the modern brain/mind.

My goal here, however, *is to re-examine the interplay between data and the conceptual framework in which it is understood.* Given the semantic slippage and reifications I note in current literature applying physical concepts that objectify mental processes like consciousness or Self, I find it necessary to reorient the language and lens *altogether* and define my approach by laying down core principles for a broad conceptual paradigm for the living, based on what all life engages in to survive. Trying to quantify the laws of semiosis in the subjective experience of neural coding is a thankless enterprise since qualities of experience are unique to every organism. We need other ways of thinking, new more inclusive paradigms for patterns of sensory-information that are filtered through signifying processes at multiple systemic levels.

Brief overview of the literature

A word about method: it is justified, in my opinion, to adopt conceptual inference from analysis and synthesis founded on solid data from multiple sources in the reconstruction of early hominid mental evolution. Accordingly, against a background in the arts, humanities, and psychoanalysis, I draw, from an ample interdisciplinary palette, each field's outstanding scholarship and points. Many years of my own psychoanalytic research and writings were based on readings in human development, the philosophy of science (Hanson, 1958; Kuhn, 1962) and of language (Goodman 1984), paleo-anthropology (Marshak, 1972; Anati, 2002a&b) and the literature of semiotics. Now I embark on a new range of research topics. Entrance into an evolutionary dimension necessitated readings in the cognitive- and evolutionary-neurosciences, the emotions, comparative psychology, dialogics (Bakhtin, 1997) and psycho-history, culling ideas from the Biosemiotic literature (Lottman, 1922/1990; Hofmeyer, 1993; Deacon, 1997; Cobley Ed., 2010; Favareau, 2010, 2015; Kull, 2014; Emmeche, 2004, 2013) more basically organized and grounded in the entire Barbierian (2006–2018) theoretical opus and framework.

Predominant, by far, were books in the neurosciences, especially from cognitive, developmental, and evolutionary points of view, here sub-grouped as; those addressing the brain-mind relationship (Schwarz & Begley, 2002; Edelman, 1992; Damasio,1994,1999), those looking for consciousness (Penfield, 1975; Dehaene, 2014; Damasio, 2010; Gazzaniga, 2018), attempting to pinpoint Darwinian neural codes of consciousness (Calvin, 1996, 1998), and the bio-cognitive neuroscientists (Feldman, 2008; Gallese, 2001; 2003, 2007, 2008; Gallese & Lakoff, 2005), the evolutionary neuroscientists (Damasio, 2010; Eccles, 1989; Le Doux, 1996, 2019), beyond evolutionary psychology (Ellis & Solms, 2018); and the emotional brain people (Weinrich, 1980; Le Doux, 1996, 2018; Panksepp, 1998; Damasio, 1999, 2018; Panksepp & Biven, 2012; Davis & Panksepp, 2018). I am not a fan of comparative primate/human studies (de Waal, 1996; Greenspan & Shanker, 2004; Tomasello, 2019) given that the crucial human difference is not addressed! But cross-species developmental and emotion-studies are informative when referenced to psychoanalytic research and neuro-imaging on human brains. Neuroscience may never "see" consciousness or find semiosis, though some brain areas may light up as *signs* of such intra-cerebral events! Yet it remains astounding that in all these sophisticated volumes, not one considered the central role of *symbolization* on the development of mind and consciousness. More bewildering still, is that despite the new *embodied* neuroscientific evolutionary-developmental (evo-devo) approach and the integration of feelings, not *one single work* focuses on the DREAM as the very observational *portal* and entry-point *of* bio-subjectivity, as Freud foretold, possibly even the *evolutionary juncture* as body becomes mind! Images are, after all, the quickest means in formulating a concept.

Other readings included books on emotional expressions (Darwin, 1872; Izard, 1968, 1971, 1977; Ekman, 1980, 2006; Panksepp, 1998; Panksepp & Biven, 2012; Plutchick, 1980 a,b; & Kellerman, 1984); studies of Metaphor (Lakoff & Johnson, 1980; Johnson, 1987, 2007; Kövecses, 2003), iconographic meanings (Panovsky, 1963); all-embracing works of sweeping scope and impact (Ryle, 1949; Bronowski, 1973, Mitchel ed.,1980; Konner, 1982;Gardner, 1982; Tarnas, 1991; Harari, 2015), and from the great socio-biology synthesists (Lumsden & Wilson, 1983; Wilson, 1978, 1998, 2012). But the boldest testaments by far on the slow evolution of human experience, with corresponding shifts in the re-presentation of a subjective *Self* as *feeling-agent,* come from paleo-anthropologists (Marshack, 1972; Anati, 2002a7b), and the cultural and psycho-historians (Snel, 1953; Read, 1955; Jaynes, 1996) studying ancient artifacts, art, monuments, and texts, as *signifying indicators* of the status of the minds of those who created and inhabited them. Their analysis of paleolithic art, archaic relics, ancient edifices, and texts reveal that these are not just signs *about* early human minds, they *are* those minds. Our prehistoric sleeper in the Lascaux Caves lying dreaming of killing Bison, displaying a nocturnal erection, illustrates this. The sequential appearance of the Greek epic, lyric, myth, and tragedy, tell their own tales of the growing complexity of the minds of those who penned the dilemmas and deeds, delights and destinies, of their dramatis personae. The rise of narrative and historicity record the ascent of psyches that internalize and then *re-externalize* into ritual, story, picture, dream, that is, into "products" exposing what those people believed and valued at that time. Objectivity was a slow gain. Jaynes's (1996) and, especially Snel's (1953), exceptional insights into the undifferentiated state of pre- and Homeric humans, mirrors the landmark modern psychoanalytic research by Mahler *et al.* (1975) on the separation-individuation process illustrating the tight connection between cultural, interpersonal, and intrapsychic, development. Last but not least, are my own works (Aragno, 1997/2016, 2008/2016), which undergird my recent readings in current interdisciplinary scholarship.

In order to avert splitting mind from its brain-organ and both from the human central nervous system, which they regulate, I adopt the one-word brain/mind concept (after Davis & Panksepp, 2018) taking an *organismic* approach. The universal interpolation of *"signification"* in human experience starts from the get-go and is fundamental in modulating the nervous system in the formation of mind. An organismic model conceives of sensory *experience* as the signified, and mind as the signifier—in a step-wise, developmental semiotic progression that begins in the body, organically. Each level of symbolization radically alters what and how things are perceived, represented, and understood, re-arranging subjective experience. Meanings resulting from these structural re-organizations bring about changes in the very nature of sensory input, mode of thought, conscious understanding, and the modulation of affect and regulation of behavior (Aragno 1997/2016).

Whereas we share some sub-cortical and brainstem systems with other mammals, only humans have this cortically-enabled proclivity to "tag" experience by *naming* it. We ourselves are the generators of what we single out and isolate to see, creators and users of our signs, makers of our models, within constrained semantic frames of reference and conceptual paradigms. In order to uncover the evolutionary path from organic/molecular coding to neural-cerebral-processes of *mind* in culture, we must begin by grasping the overall functional impact of the ways we organize experience and observe: an epistemology of "gnosis," of knowledge; *how* we know what we know.

It is through language and discourse that our perceptions are conditioned through semantic fields ordained societally, and cultures transmit what to see and how to view it in many coded ways. Our minds grow through interactions learned in social milieuxes that slant signification in culturally defined ways, from the beginning, conditioning ideation in pre-assigned semantic spheres and realities. What being multilingual and practicing psycho-analysis have taught me is the extraordinary malleability of the perceptual slant; the transposability of experience, even that most fervently felt, from one level into another by transcribing and reorganizing the mode of thought; that although words matter, there are many ways to name the same thing, and strong biases enter into each passionately held belief; that how you look determines what you see, and how you listen determines what you will hear. This epistemological realization should alert us: we must be less interested in *what* we know than *how* we know it. Frames of reference organize observations, so it is essential to generate referential perspectives appropriate to the categories we study.

Seeds, cells and Sapiens, all have something in common, they cannot live in isolation; they all *inter-act* with environments, elements, bodies, people, to survive. They all require nutrients; grow, mature, generate, degenerate, and die, in the arc of life. Unlike the fixed cause-effect laws of physics, the process-dynamics of the living are always *inter-actional*, fluid, heterogenous, uneven, outcomes unpredictable; the organism's goal in self-regulation, to maintain a steady-state. The conceptual language used to study coding processes at all levels of organismic hierarchy must fit the phenomena. Different types of *inter-action* are what happen *between* living things, from molecules to neurons, organic to cultural: To understand how these derive from and generate reciprocal impact, we may study their *forms*. Principles of *form and transforming organizations* are the scientific "laws" for living systems. I propose taking a *functional* approach to the study of *all forms of inter-action*, reconceptualizing "inter-action" as the central, essential, feature of organic Life. What lives—interacts. Survival is *contingent* on interactions of different kinds. This enables us, *without* objectifying information or communication, to ask important questions like: *How* does it interact? What type of interaction is it? Does it involve a receptor, a translator, or an interpreter? What is its *functional form*? Is it a codifier, a trigger, a stimulus, a signal, a sign? And finally, a word about "information": It is quite impossible to detach *kinds* of information from their sources of conveyance and reception. So that the transmission of information in interactions, whether between molecules, neurons, organisms expressing signals, or people speaking in words, is inextricably tethered to the nature and limitations of the attributes of those systems. In other words, "information" is not an *entity* apart from its conveyance.

General Principles for an evolutionary/developmental (evo-devo) approach to the natural history of semiosis within the overarching Barbierian framework of three macro-evolutionary shifts; Organic, Neural, and Cultural codes

1. Inter-systemic Causality, refers to the interplay of impacts encroaching from many systems, externally and internally, in adaptive outcomes generated by reciprocal inter-actions at multiple levels of organization.

2. Epigenesis and Morphogenesis, as core bio-psychological evolutionary and developmental principles: **Epigenesis** refers to how earlier structures are superseded by later-developed organizations but remain active and may resurface in regression. **Morphogenesis** refers to fundamental patterns of growth and change in the living: whereas *form determines function* in the physical sciences, transformations in *functional-form* are what determine *mental-organization* in semiotic development, yielding hierarchical models. Both principles are mirrored in brain architecture. Cerebral interconnections with reciprocal projections, even those with long-distance axons, are continuously being modified: bottom up, top down, the brain functions synergistically as a whole with specialized parts.

3. The Concepts of Developmental Lines and Organization: like all growth, mental development is not uniform; each function has its *own* developmental line in accordance with its own principles. *Organization* refers to relatively stable levels or plains of mental/cognitive organization, each determined by its functional/form in a layered developmental hierarchy from simple to increasingly complex, requiring many nested levels of analysis. Favoring parsimony of cerebral-energy expenditure in cognition and communication, the enormous adaptive advantage in semiotic development, is expressed in a drive toward compression and density of meanings found in higher forms of symbolic abstraction.

4. Principles of Parsimony, Preservation, and Probability refer to evolutionary tendencies to increase expediency and efficiency in energy-reduction *and* preservation of indispensable mechanisms. The coagulation in memory of perception and affect in tightly condensed schemas of subjective experience exemplifies **Parsimony** and the efficiency of coding mechanisms preserved at all levels of organismic functioning is implemented by semiotic vehicles. **Probability** applies to human subjectivity, harkening to the quantum subject/object principle of *observational interference,* insofar as all human understanding is interpretive, highly constrained, and multi-determined by contextual conditions, intent, and cognitive means.

5. Threshold- and Phase-Transition Processes may be likened to windows of time that build up to critical periods wherein exposure to a new function must occur or is transformed, as in language acquisition. **Phase-transitions**, both societally and individually, lead to changes in state, level of organization, or consciousness, mirrored in shifts to higher synchronization in brain-activity. These may also occur in spontaneous auto-poetic processes of maturation prompted by biological factors in the arc of life.

6. Internalization and Externalization Processes occur and reoccur in recursive loops, accounting for the projection outward of what is internal and the internalization of what is external. We see these developmental oscillations interpersonally, intrapsychically and, via their manifest products, throughout evolutionary history.

7. The Aesthetic Dimension ought to be given far greater importance. The visual, plastic, dramatic and literary arts, play a huge role in mental evolution and are often heralds and first manifest expressions of human consciousness. As lightning-rods to societal crisis, values, and advances, what and *how* the arts re-present in any given era are an inroad into the collective mind and especially the creative imagination of those living in it.

8. Unique Hominid Attributes and Advantages Upright posture and bipedalism, freeing hands and favoring the visual sense over olfaction, thumb-to-hand relationship, facial musculature facilitating expressions of inner state, and oro-laryngeal anatomy enabling vocal dexterity, are the most obvious. But lengthy development and collective learning in group-settings undoubtedly increased cortical development evolving two human impulsions rarely mentioned: the drives to **explore** and to **invent**. Add to a desire to "wander," an attribute that may have spurred these, the speculative ability to "wonder": *awe*, is unique to our species and emerges early.

9. Finally, the later development of **Discourse and Dialogue** generate *semantic fields* (Lottman's semiosphere) of specific awareness: dyadic, triadic, small and large group-boundaries formed through affiliation are reinforced by discourse whereby semantic concordance cements bonds and conceptual cohesion. The roots of connectedness seed in a primal underlay that is the phylogenetic blueprint for group-affiliation. Its later development occurs through language, spoken and written. As soon as implicit ideas enter consciousness through dialogue, awareness undergoes a radical change that spreads in speech.

A word on recent studies from the neuroscientists now preoccupied with finding "consciousness": Aside from redefining and carefully differentiating diverse meanings for human "consciousness," their meticulous mappings of networks linking perception and memory provide important clues for the conceptual reconstruction of our trek to becoming consciously aware Sapiens. Perhaps due to their strict protocol in studying brain/matter, what neuroscientists do not do well is hazard an inference on what these linkages might *mean* for qualities of felt experience, the *phenomenology* of what life was like through different eras. For this, one looks to the eloquent interpretations of the cultural and psycho-historians and, by extension, as a psychoanalyst, to surmise what life *felt* like given what we now know about development and the brain.

My commitment going forward is to relate each future topic to the above principles while considering Tinbergen's (in Feldman, xiii, 2008) set of questions: How does it work? How does it improve fitness? How does it develop? How is it adaptive? Adding, most importantly; How did it evolve?

Finally, as I leave familiar shores setting out for new horizons, I approach this vast new territory undergirded by psychoanalytic knowledge from a broad developmental/evolutionary vantage-point, pursuing Freud's intuitive search for our mental "pre-history" through the portal of the bio-psychical primary process, in accordance with the coding principles of the Barbierian framework.

To be continued...

Lecture IX
Betwixt and Between
Minding the Brain

Out of the swamp of the reticular formation the cortex arose, like a sinful orchid, beautiful and guilty.

—*P Yakovlev, in, Konner 1982, p. 68*

The demand for continuity has, over large tracts of science, proved itself to possess true prophetic power.

—*W. James, 1890, p. 97*

The basic emotions are natural kinds that have specifiable neural substrates within the mammalian brain. If we do not come to terms with such foundation principles, we will have impoverished views of psychological and cultural complexities that ultimately arise form emotional learning.

—*Panksepp, 2018, p. 225*

Abstract

The three Barbierian Macro-evolutionary stages are traced in broad outlines marked by distinct manifest-shifts in semiotic advances preceded by long periods in which these developments were evolving. Within the first phase-transition, between molecular/organic coding processes and the neural codes, I ask, What came before? What is pushing evolutionary processes in the human nervous systems? And if it is new coding forms, how did they develop, and from where?

The second transition, from neural processes to natural-signal communications, I hypothesize, results as a consequence of affect-expressions at the genesis of subjectivity and "mind." The transition to iconic-signification, as in dreams, reveals the key role embodied-expressive signals have in developing human sign and representational capacities via expanded cortical/limbic interconnections unique to our species. The third transition addresses steps from iconic-signification to gestural/vocal-signs to a linguistic *system* which universally becomes cultural coin in human communication.

* * * *

Evolutionist W. James (1890) held that as new forms of being appeared, they could only be the result of a *redistribution* of original, unchanging materials. He believed that no new "natures, or factors not present at the beginning, were introduced at later stages" (p. 95). I believe that to solidify the theoretical foundations of Code Biology, it is necessary to trace the evolutionary development of semiosis considering the distinctions between various types of coding systems for different kinds of information, and to express these differences systematically. And, finally, since it is no longer possible to separate observer from observed, we are obliged to put ourselves, our senses and slant of observation, and *especially* our language, into the equation.

Nowhere is this more relevant than in the study and reconstruction of the natural history of semiosis, a process that cannot be detected even in its chief organ, the brain, and which, according to the Barbierian principle of code-poesis (2012), may well be the engine of evolution itself. In fact, tracing the natural history of semiosis may fit one of the great tenets of Freud's psychoanalytic research: that the *manifest re-presents or is an expression of latent meaning.* Like paleo-anthropologists and archeologists, we examine surface manifest remnants to infer what they say about the minds of those who left them. The real question to tackle then, is: when does semiosis become what it is, namely, *a sign taken to signify something else,* and how did it get there?

Here I begin much earlier conceptualizing each of the transition-phases leading to Barbieri's major macro-evolutionary semiotic shifts; this comprises transitions from organic codes and biological signals to differentiated feelings and natural affect-expressions; from signified mental representations to sign-markings and artifacts; and from the emergent use of vocal signals to the gradual instrumentation of crafted oro-gestural word-signs into fluent symbolic-language. Each of these exhibits different forms of transmission to convey different kinds of information.

My competence has been in the neural realm filtered through the theoretical prism of a revised developmental model of mind (Aragno, 1991/2016) based on stages of semiotic development beginning at birth. In particular, I have focused on the "dream" as bridge between body and mind, and portal into earlier modes of thought. But here I go further back, to the genesis of "mind," when things *felt in the body* became registered in cortical regions now sufficiently connected to *re-present* felt sense-experience by the brain. So, even earlier. The growth of the cortex brings not only a major organizational change—from which sprout growth-spurts in limbic, memory, and emotion-system-circuitry—but these expanding functions create and impact on an increasingly complex organism with synergistically operating interconnections from brainstem and subcortical regions to the human cortex. This synergy changes *everything;* motivation, action, inter-action, communication, and thought.

Organizing these ideas, I lean on three of the evolutionary processes and principles underlying the paradigm shift I proposed last year: these are:

5. Thresholds—likened to windows of time that have built up to a critical period wherein a new function occurs, or is transformed, as in language acquisition; and **Phase-Transition Processes**, that organically, individually and societally, lead to changes in state and level of psychical organization, mirrored in higher synchronization in brain-activity. These may also occur spontaneously prompted by biological factors in the arc of life.

6. Internalization and Externalization—processes that occur and reoccur in recursive loops, accounting for the projection outward of what is internal and the internalization of what is external. We see these developmental oscillations interpersonally, intrapsychically and, via their manifest products, throughout evolutionary history.

Both concepts of **threshold-transition** and the reciprocal feedback loops of **internalization and externalization** are of great importance in human mental development, especially psychologically. Manifestations of these processes are evident in ancient cultural reliquiae and texts and are echoed at breakthrough moments in psychoanalysis as well. But in the following I burrow into prehistory and posit where, how, and in what way, the origins of feelings and emotions became 'visibly expressed' and how these evolving expressive configurations subsequently come to be signified in imagery. Prehistoric hominids, like all animals, were motivated by survival needs and basic drives, prompted to action instinctually by the body. Yet, hominids gradually differentiate from all other species by virtue of certain anatomical and cerebral advantages, elaborated and reinforced over millennia. To understand just how *embodied* our ancient drives and feelings were at the outset we have to speculate from the dawn of Habilis how increasing neural feedback loops evolved and grew, reinforcing connections from body to brain and back.

Simply stated: I believe there was a point in the evolution of the human nervous system when visceral-bodily feelings interwove with the brain, specifically, via the "old interior," our "brain in the gut" generated by the neuronal impact of the all-important Enteric Nervous system. At this point, feelings beyond instinctual drives started to be *felt* and, gradually, after a certain neural threshold was reached, became externalized in embodied expressions, and "seen." My hypothesis posits that these cortically-dependent emotive and visual stimuli might also have subsequently yielded the advancement from organic-signal to sign-functions: i.e., that emotional-expressions are the wellsprings at the genesis of neural semiosis building on a unique trait belonging to our species; the assignment, recognition, and creation, of *meaning*.

It seems to me that the first *meanings* were *feelings*. And feelings are "felt" in the body: How then did they get to the brain? In drawing a parallel between how proteins are formed when amino acids bond in a specific sequence, Barbieri (2015) writes, "feelings come into being when events that occur *separately* in the body and the brain are somehow brought together into a single experience" (p. 124). It is that "somehow brought together" that I address here.

The Enteric Nervous System

As a preeminent neuroscientist interested in emotions, A. Damasio has been writing about feelings since the 1990s but only recently (2018) has he begun to draw attention to the "neglected role of the gut" (p. 133). Much of the neurological data that follows is from Damasio's (2018, pp. 128–138) account. Despite their rigorous research, however, neuroscientists are loathe to venture into inferential analysis regarding what their data might mean in the bigger picture. For this, one must be willing to go to a "bigger picture" risking a leap in conceptual synthesis by a series of widening "generalizing abstraction," something S. Langer (1967, p. 153) extoled for its conceptual benefits.

My question is: How did feelings become visually expressed? And my hypothesis begins with an assumption: that "communication" within small groups would have been of supreme survival value for early hominids so that the gradual externalization of inner "feeling" and intent, accompanied by expressive sounds, would have been foremost in early communication. Inasmuch as many of our primate cousins, and other animal-species, communicate state and intentions via visually and audibly powerful physical signals, we may confidently assert that our given repertoire of basic emotional-expressions are innate and among the firmest phylogenetically secured of universal human characteristics. (see Darwin, 1872; Izard, 1968; 1971, 1977; Plutchik, 1980a, 1984; Panksepp, 2012; De Waal, 1996; Damasio, 1999; 2010, 2018; Solms 2020, 2021; Le Doux, 1996, 2019; Weinrich, 1980). I have suggested referring to the basic repertoire of universal affect-expressions as natural *affects* while restricting the term *emotions* to the more subtle, differentiated states acquired during development, and learned within specific cultures. This distinction helps differentiate the primal, unregulated cries of raw untutored affects from more complex, elaborate emotions. That said, the question remains: How did they first appear expressively? A quick overview of the human nervous system *in toto* is in order for my account to be complete.

The human nervous system has central and peripheral components. Its main organ, the cerebrum/brain, contains two hemispheres connected by a *corpus callosum,* enveloped by *the cerebral cortex* divided into lobes. The cortex also includes a region visible only on the internal (mesial) surface called the *cingulate cortex*, two non-visible regions deep under the frontal parietal lobe, and the *insular cortex* and *hippocampus* (all important for memory) hidden in the temporal lobe. Deeper underneath, are a conglomerate of nuclei, the *basal ganglia, amygdala, diencephalon, thalamus, and hypothalamus,* the last closer to the brainstem with which it shares vital functions in life regulation.

The central nervous system (CNS) connects all parts of the body to the brain in feedback loops, through bundles of axons (nerves) the aggregate of which constitute the *peripheral nervous system*. But not all are purely neural. In particular, the peripheral conveyances related to emotional *feelings* are also *humoral*, involving chemical signals travelling in blood capillaries that penetrate areas of the nervous system devoid of the blood-brain barrier; the brainstem, higher telencephalon, and dorsal root ganglia, primitive areas that receive these chemical-signals *directly*. The dorsal root ganglia, in fact, gather together cell-bodies of neurons whose axons distribute widely in viscera sending body-signals to the CNS. Loopholes are areas without the blood-brain barrier where the body's influence is *direct* via chemical molecules exerting their impact through the brainstem to the cortices. Sensory channels and *feeling* channels are quite different in kind.

One of the oldest parts, mostly outside volitional control, and crucial for its role in life-regulation, is the *autonomic nervous system*, consisting of the *sympathetic, parasympathetic,* and *enteric nervous systems*, the last of *paramount* importance here for its critical role in feelings and emotions. However, far from peripheral, the enteric nervous system may well be *central*, second only to the brain in structural and functional importance.

Believed to antedate the central nervous system, the enormous Enteric Nervous System contains an estimated 100–600 million intrinsic neurons that connect to higher brain centers through the vagus nerve, and is now thought to be instrumental in affecting mood and state. Its enormous number of neurons (equaling or more than the spinal cord), and its autonomous functioning, make it a sort of second "gut-brain," which may well be atop the *feeling* chain of command going *to* (not *from*) the brain. The brain can, however, modulate its functioning. Fibers of the vagus nerve, our main conduit of neural signals from thorax and abdomen to the brain, are mostly unmyelinated. This means that their impulses can be conveyed laterally providing opportunistic shortcuts in generating feelings (Damasio, 2018, p. 132), also suggesting that they originate from earlier times. Given all of this, and if the earliest organisms were simple tubes for ingesting nutrients and excreting waste, it is not farfetched to speculate that the ancient enteric nervous system may indeed have been the "first" brain. Moreover, at the experiential level, all early life and care is closely associated with ingestion and excretion. When we feel emotions like grief, fear, anger, elation, we feel them in the gut, disrupting appetite and digestion, making their registration and regulation critical for the homeostatic role they play throughout life, especially during development. More so in ancient humans, as they were probably less modulated, still closely tied to instinctual drives, strong affects, and vital needs. This aligns me with the James/Lange theory of emotions, which argued that emotions are a *consequence* rather than the cause of the bodily experience associated with their expression.

Here the key roles of memory and imitative learning play an influential role: From vague stirrings of proprioception would have grown, of necessity, the coevolution of exteroceptive/interoceptive senses along with intensely felt affects, reinforcing attention and memory, impacting dramatically on mental imaging while helping to expand the all-important human neocortex. Upright posture and increasing bipedal mobility in Habilis would have required memorizing route, place, person, and process, reinforcing what starts immediately in facial recognition. And from the cortex begins new learning. This would have engaged small children very early in imitative learning; facial and gestural mimicry at first growing into learning-proper in conduct and necessary skills in group collaboration. This puts imitative learning at the forefront of early human development.

In fact, the discovery of the "mirror neuron" networks (Rizzolati, Fogassi, & Gallese, 2001) attests to a resonance-circuitry, shared with primate cousins, undergirding innate imitative and empathic behaviors. Gallese (2001, 2003) proposed this "embodied simulation" to be a *sub-personal* level instantiation of several circuits that accompany multilevel changes in body states. Rooted in substrate lying just below language areas, the mirror neurons are believed to scaffold higher cognitive connections, even abstraction, in a "shared manifold" engendering imitation and empathic (identificatory?) behaviors (Gallese, 2003, p. 177). Along with kinetic imitation, mental imaging (the mind's eye) would have further enhanced visual recall of experiences forming dynamic-schemas of all kinds.

As with most in the animal kingdom, the roles of imitative learning and play dominate early childhood. But in humans there are added dimensions; the famous peekaboo game, initially a test of a toddler's object-constancy, and *imagination*, introducing the "pretend" or "*as if*" dimension to play, games, and storying. Both build on cortical functions; the ability to retain an object in the mind's eye and to discern between real and pretend. Along with the growth of short- and long-term memory, the accretion of inner-picturing underscores how representational-processes, first learned in imitation, now layer over primitive affect-*schemas* with ever more articulate gestural/ linguistic signifiers adding to the mix.

Importantly, distinctions need to be made in gradations from earlier to later forms of our image/representation function, especially considering that the origin and development of this capacity is functionally dependent on the cortex, a surface area that evolved very slowly. Initially, experience would have been highly subjective, as it is at the start of life, limited to primary needs; the primary goals of primitive life are governed by survival, food, water, shelter, procreation, proximity. Once registration and expression of feelings began to have more *meaning*, communication and collaboration in extended group-relations would have become prominent and more complex, adding to the stimulus load. Now the dynamics of context become all-important. This daily inpouring of impressions may, in part, be processed consciously in habitual situations that are familiar and relatively conflict-free. But not completely; dreaming filters and metabolizes stimuli working on unresolved issues unconsciously where subjectivity is expressed without bias. So, tirelessly, we continue our processing-work outside awareness. This condensation of experiences in imagery, layered by memory-systems, is observable in dreams where current impressions conflate with the past, emotions couple with perceptions conjuring composite pictographs, and desire is given visible form.

Dreams are a valuable window through which to see how signification takes shape. Our most fascinating and fantastical natural mental product, they shift effortlessly on the cusp between feeling, remembering, experiencing, and depicting, in a deep *un*conscious state displaying a unique vocabulary spun out of subjective experience. Both portal into and bridge from body to mind, dreams exhibit in *statu nascendi* how felt-ideas coagulate into condensed images in timeless, personal dreamscapes. A neural passageway like a processing plant, dreams are creative patchworks, constructed out of fleeting impressions, memories, and current feelings, wrought into elements revealing how meanings form according to a hierarchy of emotional and regulatory strategies, nurtured by cognition and imagination. Dreams garner their immense power by encapsulating idea, feeling, and meaning, instantaneously. Their imagery expresses *embodied* cognition; the *form* of a *felt-idea* bursting directly from *gut*-intelligence.

The dream's manifest/latent two-tiered semiotic structure, based on metaphorical and metonymic processes, is *central* to all human cognition and continues issuing from a sensorimotor matrix throughout life. At the core "umbilicus" (Freud 1900) of every dream are its latent "ideas"; and it *is these* that are expressed through manifest-content imagery, narratized by way of a "secondary revision" that constructs a storyline through sequential verbal recounting. Via the dreamer's fragmentary comments and associations, we unpack the sources and multiple meanings condensed in each element, and, through their transcription into language, we move from Unconscious, Preconscious, to Conscious awareness; from neuronal-transmission, to felt/icon, to denotive referencing, uncovering the laws of *meaning*. The information dreams provide is exactly what is going on in *that* mind; and the phenomena they expose, are *how* this is being processed by strategizing how to deal with it.

Renown for his studies of forebrain functioning during dreaming, the neurology of dream-sleep laid out by M. Solms confirms many of Freud's insights. (*I am deeply indebted to M. Solms for his clarifying answers to all my questions, and his invaluable input in a series of personal email exchanges during 2021*). The dream-process is driven by subcortical, mesocortical/mesolimbic dopamine circuitry, in particular. Its motivating spark "the Wish," issues from an upsurge of limbic and basal ganglionic activity, structures responsible for drives, affects and autobiographical memory (hippocampus) and, whereas the prefrontal lobes are partly deactivated during sleep, the posterior cortex remains activate in dreaming. Solms (2021) views this as the physiological correlate of a topographical regression since, "What is older in time is more primitive in form and... in psychical topography lies nearer to the perceptual end" (Freud,1900, p. 548). Freud called this Ucs "mode of thought" the *primary process,* and the complicated process by which the dream's core *thoughts* are portrayed in imagery he called the "dream-work." During the dream's formal regression, the earlier form is revived, whereby "...*the fabric of the dream-thoughts is resolved into its raw material*" (Freud, p. 543). Interpreting dreams through the linguistic *secondary process,* we unpack meanings that are condensed into image-elements via profuse associations, uncovering a semiotic sequence that recapitulates a sign-referential course towards conscious awareness.

The importance of Freud's theory of dream interpretation is this: it presents a microcosm of two transitions; the first, when sensory/emotive input and impulses merge with mnemonic-processes generating "primary process" signified-pictographs in *figurative form*; the second, when these image-elements are unpacked and translated interpretively through the cultural medium of language in *verbal form*. These two transformations—the first a trans*figuration* from senses and emotions into image, the second, a transposition in sign-*form*, from image into language (icon into verbal-sign), illustrate a semiotic sequence that recapitulates the gradual accretion of conscious awareness through the use of signs and symbol systems.

Cognition began in "imaging" at a phase in mnemonic development when raw affects and basic needs predominate, generating composite imagery of what was *felt* with what was seen, in dynamic schemas in the mind's eye. This differs from later, more complex and elaborate sign *re-presentations* conveying meanings that have been filtered through semiotic *instruments,* i.e., learned signals, signs, and symbols, expressing subjectivity but also including and integrating greater aspects of culturally acquired signs and learned behaviors.

We would be at a loss to even begin interpreting the multiple-meanings encased in dreams, without Freud's basic (1900) dictionary for their composite meaning-forms; and we would be unable to articulate or communicate our interpretations of their meanings without an efficient common-language medium. Ah! the linguistic code! Our primary universal cultural tool, communicative medium, instrument of reason, reflection, and thought, our inner companion and internal guide. Language not only enables us to express our thoughts and ideas but creates the verbal glue that binds and bonds us to our group and society. More even than home or land, our mother-tongue forms the deepest part of our identity, early on, stringing together a core biographical memory rooted in our origins.

It is hard not to conceive of a slow developing progression from early hominid embodied communication in primitive expressive-signal-calls, to more discrete single-word-signs encompassing personal names, objects, and processes, to a gradual stringing together of more and more word-labels into syntactical chains. The propulsion of recounting and story-telling invites phrases to add adjectival embellishments in a concatenation of "and thens," and even the basic "sentence" promotes a declaration of desire or intent in the formulation of a thought. And so, this phase-transition, from the advent of neural codes to the establishment of cultural codes, would have been spurred by interactions uttered in small hominid groups in the pursuit of a primary need to devise the most efficient, expedient, and parsimonious mode for communicating—a common language.

In sum; by asking what came before, and hypothesizing the "in betweens," I have laid out possible micro-evolutionary stages leading up to each of the three major Barbierian macroevolutionary shifts, positing: 1. that innate affect-expressions emerged from the transmission of feelings originating in the primal enteric nervous system; 2. that affect-expressions would have gradually differentiated, becoming labeled by vocal-signs that expanded interactions via embodied oro-gestural forms of communication, and; 3. that from persistent use of signs in different media would have evolved a syntactically structured culture-specific linguistic form of communication. This evolutionary progression from organic to felt affect-signals, to the use of embodied signs, to cultural symbol systems, mirrors the stratified development of the human brain, each phase prompted by the developed employment of a new form of coding device.

To be continued...

Lecture X
Referencing Meaning Matters

Meaning... is the inevitable product of a code because there cannot be codes without meaning or meaning without codes.

—Barbieri, M. 2003/2019, p. 9.

...meaning arises from embodiment as a unit of referential interactions.

—G. M. Edelman, 1992, 152.

Abstract

This talk asks: What is *"meaning"*? How best can we define or study "it"? Is code-form sufficient in itself to have "meaning," or is it that once decoded we have assigned meaning to it; and if molecular codes have meaning, what kind of meaning is it? What constitutive essentials define a meaning as *human*? These questions touch on one of the most tricky and problematic points of the Barbierian code-driven macro-evolutionary paradigm.

Deeper exploration of this insufficiently examined subject and loosely used term is sorely needed. I enter this vast territory of investigation from a new critical vantage-point, continuing to unify the biological with the psychological in the Freudian tradition.

My bi-directional analysis of the structure of "meanings" in relation to coding-types takes its point of entry by questioning and contrasting the two above quotes with respect to a "referential hierarchy," going on to pinpoint the nature of information that each level of code/semiotic-form is designed to carry, and how it is transmitted. This leads to the question: What is the mode and *functional-form* of conveyance by which "signification" is effectuated, since it is through their *form* in relation to different systems of signs that "meanings" are created and apprehended?

115

This brief exploration of a large topic redefines the inquiry through an examination of its diverse forms *in interaction,* at multiple levels of systemic organization and development. Analogous to Poppers three worlds, Barbieri's three-phase evolutionary framework of Organic, Neural, and Cultural Codes, is examined from molecular to verbal communication. Each level is addressed considering the core principles guiding the developmental/ evolutionary approach previously presented with the ideal of eventually systematizing a typology of meaning-forms.

* * * *

> As living beings, we have a built-in drive to make sense of the world, to give meanings to things and when we give meaning to something, that something becomes a sign for us. Sign and meaning, in other words, cannot be taken apart, because they are two sides of the same coin.
> —*M. Barbieri, 2008, p. 25*

Meaning is neither "thing" nor abstraction; it is not caused, yet certainly has effects. It arises in interactions transmitting information of different kinds, yet it is not information. How, then, is meaning made? What are its essential constitutive factors? What types of interaction determine the presence of meaning? Considering its complexity, how do we even approach such a slippery subject?

I begin with a basic premise; that meaning is engendered through diverse interactions along a hierarchy of transmissive processes, from embryonic to increasingly complex. Coding and decoding meanings at all levels of this hierarchy, from organic to cultural, implies that, at times meaning is intended, at others we ourselves assign it. It is customary to pair meaning with semiosis in that *signification* is the assignation of meaning. But this definition breaks down at the molecular/organic level. Barbieri (2008) nevertheless gets around this specifying: "A semiotic system is always made of signs and meanings that are linked together by the components of a third party, but this party can be of three different types: (1) an external codemaker, (2) an internal interpreter and (3) an internal codemaker" (p. 25).

Many things enter into the creation and reception of meanings, including context, semantic reference and, especially, overall mental organization, which determines the intended meaning and how it is deciphered or interpreted. The question then becomes: What are the constitutive differences in interactions between organic, neural, and cultural coding modes, which leads to an examination of their forms at these different systemic levels.

Beginning at the beginning: The Genetic Code. *Making life.*

The question of how life on earth began has been asked since the dawn of science, from Aristotle's "life begets life" to "matter begets life," to chemistry, taking us to a time well before 3.5 billion years ago, to the first fossil records. Speculations have it that it all begins in murky primordial waters teaming with iron, sulphur, nitrogen and ammonia, minerals from nearby volcanos, perhaps charged by a lightning strike. This chemical/mineral mixture provides building blocks for the first protocells, bacteria, and single-cell microorganisms, to form and swim about, equipped only with sense-responses to their environment. One day conditions were propitious for a catalytic event bringing one such primitive microorganism to stick and bond to another, producing the first replication. And the rest is the history of the relentless forward march of evolution, producing more replications and species-diversification through selection and adaptation.

Fast forward to the mid-1900s when rapid advances in molecular biology were made in deciphering the microprocesses of life, culminating with the cracking of the double helix of the genetic code in 1953. Today, microbiologists argue whether it was the single-strand RNA (among the most ancient of molecules) or the double-strand DNA that jump-started this burst of life-propagation. But all agree on the extraordinarily complex precise mechanisms of microcellular replication. The deciphering of DNA uncovered a molecular coding process within and between cells that, in all appearance, resembles and functions like a semiotic system. Its means of interacting is by transmitting information via RNA messenger carriers, hence, the "genetic code" with its minimalist alphabet, ACGT, for Adenine, Cytosine, Guanine, and Thymine, the chemicals that make up its nucleotide base. These chemicals carry transcribed instructions telling the cell how to make a specific protein. The language used to describe the cell is one of self-organizing molecular "machinery," a rule-based artifact-making "factory." Not only does the coding of life spell its chemical-letters, but their sequencing is crucial. Change one (among millions) in a copying error, and you have a mutation.

The discovery of the genetic code made it clear to some theoretical biologists that life originates from, and depends, on chemistry *as well as* organic coding processes, of which more specific ones are being discovered all the time; "the living world is literally teeming with organic codes" (Barbieri, 2011, p. 370). Yet mainstream biology sticks to the chemical theory, taking little note of the implications of finding that coding sequences and signal-transfers associated with higher cerebral processes originate in precursors at molecular levels.

In several books and many papers, the founder and leading exponent of a code-based evolutionary theory, M. Barbieri, goes to great lengths to explain the claims of Code Biology differentiating it from other groups adhering to partial theories or inapplicable definitions of organic semiosis. He writes that the discovery of biological information transformed biochemistry into molecular biology, pinpointing the "nature of sequence information" as "the key issue" (2015, p. 8) amplifying the classical paradigm, *"life is chemistry"* to *"life is chemistry-plus-information"* (p. 9). Due to the fundamental contribution Barbieri's model advances regarding the centrality of the cell's "code-maker" function, he adds, that life is *"chemistry-plus-information-plus coding"* (2015, p.19). Question: How does meaning enter into this?

I am unable to repeat Barbieri's detailed explanations advocating for his code-based arguments; suffice it to say they appear convincing. Until, that is, we arrive at an analysis of "meaning." Let us begin then with an oft-cited Barbierian definition compiled from several writings: "A code is a set of rules implemented by 'adaptors' establishing a correspondence between two independent worlds, . . . a mapping between signs and meaning" (Barbieri, 2003, 2019). Likening the correspondence between "A" and "dot-dash" of the Morse code to saying that "dot-dash" is *the meaning* of "A," he states, "Meaning . . . is the inevitable product of a code . . . there cannot be codes without meaning or meaning without codes" specifying that meaning is a "mental entity" when it is between mental objects but an "organic entity" when between organic molecules (2019). Aside from the problematic use of "entity" (noun) to define an interactive co-constructed process of information-transmission, "information" ought not be equated with "meaning" insofar as it does not specify *what* that information *means*.

Given the common understanding that *signification*, by definition, is contingent on something being taken to represent something else, and even granting that we must now scale back the proto-origins of *semiosis* to begin at microbiological levels, let us look closer at the consequence, or even necessity, of stretching the meaning of meaning so far! Take, for example, the RNA messenger that transmits the coded DNA instructions: here the messenger *is* the message, neither reference or meaning apply. Or the "dot-dash" as "A," of the Morse code: here "dot dash" does *not mean* A, it *corresponds to* A, one letter in words composed of several more. This one-to-one structure presents an *equivalency*; it *equates with*, no distance whatsoever between code-sign and referent, no meaning implied. In fact, I fail to understand why meaning means so much to Barbieri, or is even desirable, since his code-based theory of macro-evolutionary shifts would remain unscathed if molecular *meaning* was dropped altogether. Coding mechanisms do not need meaning to remain the root-source of all ascending more complex forms of semiosis. Given the one-to-one equivalence of coded form, it is far less ambiguous than more elaborate semiotic systems *with* reference since it eliminates "sense"[1] and this actually supports the claim that the early genetic code was imperfect, still ambiguous, only in time solidifying its invariant structure.

In my committtment to include the contributions of observer to the obeserved I would say that regarding molecular codes, "meaning" rests in the eye of the beholder. We describe from a vocabulary of patternings with which we are already familiar, but in so doing *assign* rather than *find* inherent meaning in them. Moreover, Barbieri's statement that the "*elementary* act of semiosis is a triad of *"sign, meaning and convention"* (Barbieri, 2015, p. 30) would *exclude* unconscious meanings which are idiosyncratic, embodied, and follow no convention. Code-form *per se* carries no "meaning" and this has nothing to do with "interpretation" or its absence; it has to do with its *form*. Yet the *seeds* of semiosis still rest in the molecular code-formations

---

1 In support of the distinction between two types of meaning, Barbieri invokes Frege's (1892) ideas on 'sense and reference' regarding internal and external meanings (1915, pp. 164–165), an argument that given today's advancements in the philosophy of language appears outdated and unconvincing.

that transcribe and transmit chemical information.What is eminently valuable in the overall Code-based theoretical framework is locating the sourcepoint *of all* semiotic forms building above it in the self-generative and *reproductive processes* that originate life, processes that evolved to no other end than to reproduce themselves (Olds, 2000).

The Second Macroevelutionary Shift. Neural Codes.
Making Human Meanings

Dreams think predominantly in images.
—*Freud, 1900, p. 49*

Fast forward billions more years: From primitive crude senses, to a nervous system based on a reflex arc, there are now many diverse multicellullar animal species with complex nervous-systems roaming around the earth. Each species is genetically endowed with instinctive reaction-patterns specific to its adaptational fitness, reproduction, and survival needs; animals are driven by instincts; hominids, more and more, by *purpose*. Human evolution advanced gradually *pari passu* with a growing neocortex and limbic system. We are now tracing the bio-cogntive means by which *only* hominids could have elaborated strictly *human meanings*. In this, skulls, cerebral architecture, and resulting sensory processing, tell their own story through changing gait, size, and shape.

Approximately 4 1/2 to 5 million years ago, the *Homo* genus and higher primates separated from common ancestors. From Australopithecine A., already upright, bipedal, but with a small brain, through tool-using and culture-dependent *H. Habilis,* with only slightly larger brains, then between *H. Erectus* and *H. Sapiens,* an astounding doubling of the brain occurs. Overall, cranial size tripled over three million years, implying that, in each successive species, a major reorganization of the nervous system occured, favoring skill over strength in conferring adaptive ascendance. Of the five senses, sight is now the most important. Locomotor efficiency, perceptual acuity, precision-grip manual-dexterity, communal living, and proto-lingustic gestural and vocal articulations evolved alongside premature

120

births, due to narrowing of the femle pelvis, so, better parenting, perhaps stronger bonds.

All of this explains why language areas, and a brief window of time to acquire speech, as well as seven or *eight primary emotional expressions* with pervasive neuro-physiological impact, are phylogenetically hardwired.

This remarkable increase in brain-size, not only in neocortical learning areas, but also in limbic mnemonic and affect cerebellar regions, increases motor and associational pathways that *interconnect the whole brain and nervous system.* With increased perceptual acuity, and geared for action, there would have developed a downward cascade from the cortex with feedback from peripheral receptors firing up and down the spinal cord initiating *proprioception* (self-awareness in time and space) and *interoception* (awareness of one's states and feelings) originating in the enteric nervous system. Predominance of visual, motor, and emotional sensory processing make *subjective-experience* prominent in the reorganization of the nervous system. At this point, "dynamic schemas," as neuronal clusterings, would have begun recording and encoding entire scenarios. And from this "proto-self," the people, sounds, interactions, places, and events in daily life reinforce mnemonic-engrams, impacting all cerebral/mental development. The intensification of subjective-experience, learning, and communication, would have created a burst in representational abilities.

But with all this increasing barrage of proprioceptive, social, and sensory stimuli to sort and integrate by a central control system, how did our ancestors cope? The taxed hominid brain now extends its hours, working a double shift, into the night! Enter the *dream!* Unable to externalize impulse in action, the brain begins to hallucinate to itself its thinking in images culled and collated from layers of impressions and experiences, past and recent. *No one has sufficiently emphasized the significance of dreaming on the expansion of neocortical functions like sensory integration from two hemispheres, and its sequelae for strictly human faculties like imagination, anticipation, volition, agency.* As *H. sapiens* began registering feelings, and picturing thoughts in dreams, might also be when "eidetic images," verissimilitude depictions, begin appearing on cave walls. The confluence of recorded-perception and depicted-image then would coincide with the advent of subjectivity. In this way, biological pressures advance socio-cultural evolution, and vice versa, in progressive reciprocal feedback-loops, by internalizing and externalizing processes into products.

Pressure to externalize re-presentation must have been building, beginning with *H. habilis,* to *H. erectus,* to *H. sapiens,* alongside improved cogntive and technical skills as suddenly 40,000 years ago, cave art explodes all over the world. Let us wander deep into the great Hall of Bulls of the Lascuax caves, memorialized by a prehistoric artist who depicts a sleeping male (with nocturnl erection) dreaming of a speared bison, with a bird standing by, signfiying the flight of dreamlife (?). This cerebral processing of multiple stimuli and their projection into *mental* images marks the beginning of *human meanings* and, hence, the flowering of mind. Metabolizing condensations of multiple sensory-motor, visual, and emotional impressions, generates *meanings* in a purely subjective nocturnal pictographic language that remained mysterious for millenia. Herein lies the missing link decried in all my readings on evolution. *No one* from relevant fields of paleo-anthopology, evolutionary, or even psychoanalytic-neuroscience, has proposed the idea that *dreaming* is the *first* manifestation of hominid re-presentational capacities.Yet there it is! Staring out at us from the cave walls. A macroevolutionary shift, with new cerebral coding processes had begun, as *H. erectus* is becoming *H. sapiens*. But in order to decode this imagistic vocabulary a dictionary would be needed...

Fast forward to 1900: a research biologist turned neurologist, Sigmund Freud (1900), has taken the common dream as object of scientific scrutiny, deciphering its purpose, structure, vocabulary of meaning-making mechanisms, while constructing a model of mind that now includes unconscious *primary-process* cognition. The signifying semantic of this cognitive mode is *completely different* from *secondary-process* linguistic thought and rises to the forefront in regression, the arts, and sleep. In bold italics Freud (1900) declares, ***"The interpretation of dreams is the royal road to knowledge of the unconscious activities of the mind"*** (p. 608). The psychoanalytic window into dreams and their unconsciously constructed meaning-forms provides a microscope that telescopes back and down, *into* the body, to earlier stages and forms of sensory-processing and recording.

In his analysis of dream construction, Freud called this cerebral creation of meaning the "dream-work." He was adamant regarding distinctions between latent and manifest content (a semiotic relationship): the dreamwork, a "pictographic script" (Freud, 1900, p. 277), *condenses* and *displaces* the dream's core "thoughts" via four means of representation, lifting the dream-thoughts, and constructing its imagery by this "highly complicated activity of the mind" (Freud, p. 122). The whole subliminal train of thought has been concentrated onto singular ideational elements, and it *is these core ideas* that are then *presented* on the mind's proscenium in images compiled from sense-impressions (many trivial), memory fragments, visual stimuli, and recent experiences. "Ideas," then, coagulate into neural-schemas expressed in pictured nuggets by *mental-representations* manifesting through a pictorial mode of thought; and then this telling detail: The material of the latent dream-thoughts *is transcribed* into manifest-content "as a ready-made structure" (Freud, 1900, p. 445). Could *this* be the cerebral code surmised by Calvin, Dehaene, Barbieri, Eccles, and others?

Connecting the dream's formal regression to an ancestral *mode of cognition,* Freud proposed that one could equate dream-presentations with how "concepts" are formed from a number of perceptual images. We see the validity of this conjecture ontogenetically (when the advent of evocative-memory, the *internal-image,* heralds steps towards object-constancy), and again in the prehistoric script of cave art (Anati, 2002a), where the viewer is not only gripped by the artistic skill and sheer beauty of these images, but is *drawn into* multiple meanings conveyed *through them*: the swift movement of the herds, the crucial role of the hunt and lancing of animals for food, the succulent gush of warm entrails, the tensions sustained, day and night, for survival.

The verbal *interpretation* of dreams exhibits how thinking evolves from a sensory, kinetic/emotive, evocative, *imagistic* "primary-process," into the linear, denotive, socially-based conventions of a *linguistic* "secondary-process" mode of thought. A semantic of image into one of words; *omne signum ex signum, every sign comes from another sign.* Through this transcription, from unconscious pictorially presented core-ideas, into verbally *re-presented* meanings, we re-cognize the basic building blocks of *signification itself*—metaphor, metonymy, synecdoche, simile, analogy, all appropriated and reiterated in language. We witness this processing of the flood of experiences and impressions condensed from situations in waking life, organized by strategies of accommodation and action, secondarily narratized through the linear syntax of speech in dream analysis. Freud's rules for dream interpretation expose how and by which processes and tropes we transcribe body into mind, evocative image into sequence-governed linguistic meanings. The Freudian embeddedness in the unconscious primary process enables us to witness the laws of cognition and abstraction as they grew out of context-dependent, *embodied,* sensory-emotive experiences into coagulant *mental*-representations.

The Third Macroevolutionary Shift. The Cultural Code. *From Words into Language.*

A vocal sound becomes a call; a facial expression a signal; moves mold into gestures. Hominid signification evolved gradually, in stages and phases, superimposing over facial/embodied emotional-expressions ever more specific oro-gestural (Rizzini, 2015) communications familiar to those within small socio-cultural groups. In addition to carefully recorded lunar-calendric markings indicating time-factored cogntive awareness, one may infer increased indicative sounds and denotive single-vocables alongside "names" in storied-descriptives growing slowly into proto-vocabularies. From distinct calls, language would have evolved rife with expressive sounds and gestures, all of which signal meanings. But even before, nestled under our two language areas (Broca and Wernicke), are critical precursor imitative centers, the "mirror neuron" circuit, source of an exceptional primate proclivity to *learn-by-imitation.*The human child's thirst for observing, imitating and playing, starts early with delight in babbling and the first "smile" of recognition—unforgettable!

Other primates with similar attachment-drives beat humans until the magic age of three (Tomasello, 2019), when our social shared-attention, curiosity, and hunger to taste, touch, test, and try, *everything*, drastically outsmarts our primate cousins. From then on, the extraordinary neocortical capacities for learning, speaking, grasping meanings, having purposes, strategizing plans, and forming goals, i.e., the *whole panoply* of human charactertsitics explode displaying our formidable cerebral advantage.

The transitions from living in a sensorimotor, *bio-instinctually*-driven world of action/tools (*Habilis/Erectus*) into a more goal-driven *psycho-cognitively*-dominated world of crafting/creating in social groupings (*Sapiens*), reveals itself in the relics and product-remnants of these diverse evolving eras. The thresholds that led to the great burst of engravings and cave-art scripts of 40,000 years ago left extraordinary evidence for experts to peer into the human ancestral mind. Paleo-anthropologists Anati (2002a) and Marshack (1972) agree that Upper Paleolithic hominids *already* had semiotic capacities—pattern-recogntion belonging to the species—as they hunted and lived collaboratively, signalling communications through sounds and gestures. One would not expect language, our most expedient semiotic system, to sprout fully formed. Precursors of verbal signification are hard-wired, inherent in the human disposition for dynamic schematization and pattern-matching. Seeds of signification are already germinating in visual gestalt-processes of perception, in expressive gestures and tonal sounds, *long* before the first words. May we assume then that at molecular and neural levels, the predisposition for meanings exists *in potentia*, just as the acorn in no way resembles the oaktree, out of which it will grow.

Once words appeared, language would have built on itself, growing exponentially through feedback loops from social interactions-to-cognizing-mind and back, landing on syntax, the great linearizer of the storied mode. If Metaphor, the application of something familiar to something new, is the meta-code for sensory-motor experience-to-image (body to mind) in dreams, Narrative is the meta-code of language. The storying tendency seen in picture-scripts is applicable to all Time-factored proccesses, leading to consequential *outcomes*, conclusions, anticipations, the "and then" that leads implicitly to parables, moral codes, juridical codes, and into the very cogntive structures that built civilizations. This fundamentally *interactive* consideration, emphasizing the social role of communication, is very important when speculating on the co-evolution of language and mind in primordial groups and societies. Semiotic advances not only gave rise to complex meanings but to *complex minds,* assigning meanings that interweave with the accretion of ever more elaborate forms of reference and signification. In conveying "sense," one could not imagine formulating complex ideas without the vocables to express abstract concepts. Despite the great leap that languge brings to cognition, the price is a loss to the senses; conventional meanings are pale and bleached-out in the march of words casting passion and the panoply of subtle emotions of the inner life, into the non-verbal world of music, the Arts, and dreams.

The languages we speak *create* and *contain* the beliefs and values inherent in the systems of society we live in, not to mention style. They are multi-coded conduits of conduct as much as they become modified by the culture and cognizing of people in them. And the whole grows on thickly-

125

layered residues of semiotic phases that came before; ours is a polysemic world, teaming with word-ambiguities layered from etymological origins, peppered by expressive and descriptive verbal and non-verbal tropes playing with meanings containing the gamut of signals, signs, and symbols, in everyday speech. As a precision instrument to articulate conscious thought, language is unbeatable. Yet meaning, as we think of it, is always co-constructed, the implicit function of language—to convey sense.

In order to obtain the precise "sense" in which a meaning is intended, we need a referential orbit or semantic, *a context*, which leads me to the two opening quotes; one claiming meaning is implied in codes, the other, stating meaning builds on embodied reference. The first applies meaning to a molecular process that uses a coded mechanism in RNA transfer of information, viewing the cell-unit as a semiotic system: the second implies that meaning evolves from the bodied/brains of people using a linguistic referential system of words.

To summarize my opinion: I view the biological seeds of semiotic structure at the molecular level as the acorn to the Oaktree. However, tracing the evolution of the human nervous-system/brain through various epochs in neural terms, one finds that meaning requires some subjectivity and frame of reference to form. From crude emotional-expressions and oro-gestural-signals would gradually have developed more specific sound-signals and distinct sign-forms like indicative labels or names, leading to the refinement of all representational capacities unique to our species that culminate in symbolic language. *Human* meaning-forms *depend* on neuronal feedback loops from body to cortex and back to co-compose them. The communicative conveyance of meaning-making therefore requires a consensual semantic orbit, socially created, designated by specific situations by embodied people. As a personal construction, meaning is contingent on, and alters, according to the level of semiotic organization in which experience is represented.

Finally, consider the etymology of "meaning" itself: Descending from the Saxon *menian,* through Old English *maneen,* and Middle English *mēnen;* to *"intend"* **to do something,** plan, indicate an object or convey a certain sense, by the late 13th, century Old French, *mena,* joins the Greco-Latin *semeion, sign, signum, significare,* to identify, signify, to express. Not until 1827, does it become a verbal noun, *meaning, meaningful (Webster's New World Dictionary,* 1966).

We can see in its Anglo-Saxon origin just how ***embodied*** in action the roots of meaning are, whereas its Greco-Latin source refers more clearly to a semiotic structure, taking something *to mean something else*, a referential act. One wonders if, in this etymological contrast, there might be clues to the cultures themselves or to their stage of mental development, and if this says anything about the evolution of concepts. But to explore this and other related issues on human semiotic developments requires another day.

To be continued...

Lecture XI
The Tree of Representation
Bridging the Gap between Brain and Mind

This is the *code theory of mind*, the idea that there has been a *universal neural code* at the origin of mind as there has been a universal genetic code at the origin of life.

—*Barbieri, 2015*

The biological development of mapping and its direct consequence – images and minds—is an insufficiently heralded transition in evolution.
—*Damasio 2012, p. 143*

We must be prepared... to assume the existence... not only of a second unconscious, but of a third, fourth, perhaps of an unlimited number of states of consciousness, all unknown to us and to one another.
—*Freud, 1915, p. 170*

Abstract

This presentation traces epigenetic steps in the evolution of representation examining when, how, and even *why*, this neural advance would have begun in light of what evidence there is from pre-history, neuroscience, and contemporary developmental studies. Psychoanalytic research, in particular, informs of the vicissitudes in the development of this function. Through our portal into the dream's primary process meaning-making forms we infer how from sensorimotor embodied registrations other coding mechanisms would have evolved, layer by layer, adding new semiotic vehicles each with its own distinct signifying vocabulary.

This most fundamental of human cerebral faculties, that begets mind, requires a broad interdisciplinary palette to integrate into a Barbierian evolutionary framework, its many psycho-cognitive accomplishments correlating with changing kinds of internalization, mnemonic processes, and forms of meaning-making. From paleo-anthropology, we learn of its manifest embryonic beginnings; from iconography, implications for interpreting the signifying level of its images; and from neuroscience, the mapping of evolving functional circuitry connecting the old brainstem with the newer cortex. Continuing my quest in finding continuities between body and mind, this exploration concludes with the meta-codes for our tree of representation.

* * * *

Before the word was the image.
—*Read, 1955, p. 20*

Before *re*-presentation is *presentation*, the dim record of an image; and before presentation are sensorimotor/schemas, registered and recorded, *in the body*. Without the mind's eye, embodied experience leaves organic traces only; with it, there is Mind.

We begin in a diffuse blur of multisensory synesthesia. As the nervous system begins to organize and process experience, the first perceptual gestalts form. These evolve into more differentiated sensorimotor dynamic schemata of entire scenarios laying engrams that will slowly stimulate evocative memory. All senses are involved—sight, sound, touch, smell, and feelings. The effort to retain some-thing *in mind* that is absent to the senses, beginning around 18 months, will afford immeasurable adaptive advantage to a species that builds on this cognition by adopting signs through which to think and communicate. This mental act, harnessed for many kinds of sign-forms and systems, differentiates humans from all other life: that we devise, adopt, and use semiotic instruments to generate referenced meanings of the *mind*. From the Upper Paleolithic explosion of art proficiency to the private condensation of dream-imagery, from language, mathematics, and computer chips, to symphonies and space-ships, our conceptual efficiency plus knowledge has led us to the moon and back.

I posit that the ability to retain an image in the mind originates in *re-*cognition, in *re-* membering the all-important face/voice of the caretaker, from which develops the inner re-*form*ulation of experience. Here I ask how representation evolved. Beginning at the advent of the Neural Code era, this exploration traces the layered development that grows from the seedling tree of human cognition. As neural encoding progressed we encounter the beginning of subjectivity: this implicates changing forms of internalization, new mnemonic and affective-signaling expressions, and sign-usage, generating different kinds of meanings. This functional convergence reflected in modulations in behavior requires broad interdisciplinarity to integrate many new psycho-cognitive accomplishments in advancing stages of re-presentation. From psychoanalysis, I will address its interpersonal underpinnings; from paleo-anthropology, its manifest embryonic beginnings; from iconography, its implications for interpreting signifying levels of its imagery; from neuroscience, the mapping of evolving functional circuitry between body, brainstem, midbrain, and the newer cortex; and, from *Code Biology*, Barbieri (2015) writes this on first-person experiences:

> ... they are the result of complex operations where highly differentiated cells act in concert to create a physiological short-circuit between body and brain, between observer and observed, between senders and receivers of neural signals. That kind of complexity was ... the result of an evolutionary process that was set in motion when feelings and instincts started playing specific roles in animal behaviour, i.e., when the universal neural code came into being. The origin of this code ... set in motion a true biological revolution, a major transition that transformed the unconscious brain of ... ancestral animals into the feeling brain of the modern animals. The result was an absolute novelty: it was the origin of *consciousness*, the origin of *subjectivity*, the origin of *first-person* experiences, in short, the origin of *mind*. (p. 123)

As we achieve some degree of coenesthetic organization we begin to have a proto-subjective take on experiences, creating from what is "out there," an inner construct condensing sensory input while assigning to it affective valence—or *meaning*. Emotions here play a key role. Becoming a "subject," however, is no quick or easy step, and this process of separation-differentiation, assisted by ever-increasing forms of semiotic mediation, would take millennia. With it, however, also comes an awareness of *affects*, felt, and observed, implicating intense attachments and the mirror-neuron circuitry in imitative learning. Proto-subjectivity entails proprioception, feeling one's body in place and time, a right hemisphere function that is particularly prominent in both animals and humans during REM dream-sleep. Mental representation, along with empathic/kinetic imitation, in turn, will further enhance internalizing patterns of interaction and dynamic configurations of all kinds. Keep in mind that what took millennia to evolve is now accomplished in the first three years of life by which time the human infant has far surpassed our primate cousins (Tomasello, 2019).

Let me venture a reconstruction: The phases during which the Homo-line evolved, from Habilis through Erectus, with still relatively small skulls, to Sapiens with a grown cortical mantle, upright gait, manual dexterity, perceptual acuity and mobility, produced skeletal realignments of head to spinal-cord, generating neural expansions from body to brain along with changes within cerebral systems. The first records of human "signs" appear etched on rock-surfaces and calendric baton markings. This tells us that impulses to record observations start very early, perhaps in attempts at *recording or remembering* by marking something with a sign. But even before the recording of lunar cycles, routes, or hunting strategies, there is the first universal configuration we all witness—the human face. So indelible are the eyes and mouth of the facial gestalt that infants will smile at any schematic two dots and a dash visual stimulus! The residue of this impression is "physiognomic expression" a tendency to read primal emotional expressions—smile, laughter, anger, disgust, fear, and sadness—into any configuration. Soon, however, it is not *any* face, but *the* face of Mother; her vocal tone, movements, way of holding, feeding, and especially, her facial expressions, that form a primal engram of the first intense attachment figure.

R*e-presentation* and evocative memory grow out of a need to retain within this imperative attachment figure indispensable for survival. From this visual/empathic, primordial-merger, where sender and receiver unity is still intact, undisturbed by the interpolation of learned "signifiers," we trace the slow evolution from natural-expressions through oro-gestural (Rizzini, 2015) proto-verbal communication, to increasingly efficient phonological linguistic signs. And out of this undifferentiated primal dialectic come early theories of empathy (Worringer, 1908), and all ensuing branches of inquiry investigating the natural history of signification, meaning, language, and "gnosis"—*ways of knowing.* Re-presented meaning, however, begins as perceptions and feelings meet the cortex; and thanks to growing mnemonic systems, entire dynamic scenarios are recalled in a mind's eye exercised from birth to *form*ulate gestalts of subjective experience. Before sensory-emotive registrations achieve cortical "re-presentation," there is only embodied *pre*-recorded time.

The demands of bipedalism and increased mobility, beginning with Habilis in collaborative hunting and living, would have expanded mnemonic processes to memorizing route, place, and process, superimposing on what starts immediately in facial recognition. The reinforcing roles of proprioception and memory in learning within collaborative group activities would have reinforced the coevolution of exteroceptive-interoceptive senses and the need to label and communicate these, adding to innate emotional-expressions and early forms of sign-use, all impacting dramatically on *representational* functions while rapidly expanding the all-important neocortex. The growing cortex would further reinforce imitative learning in joint attention, and what began in facial and gestural mimicry would become increasingly efficient and specific with the help of semiotic instruments like rudimentary single word-signs. This movement from innate signals to oro-gestural sign-use, accompanied by sequenced task-processes in collective activities, and especially dramatized storytelling, puts imitative learning in group-living at the forefront of early hominid development.

Today's "neuro-mapping and imaging" techniques neglect *re-presentation,* especially the distinctions between early less differentiated stages of *presentational* functions and later more developed ones. Their overly-broad designation overlooks the former, which accentuates perceptual, iconic similarities, versus the latter, which becomes overlaid by semiotic instruments and abstractions. Beginning with simple dynamic-schemas emphasizing perceptual input, mnemonic processes move to increasingly complex *re*-presentations of whole dynamic situations, as in dreams, where current experience links with layered *memories* constructing imagery driven by strong affects (hippocampal, limbic nuclei) charged with multiple *meanings*. Nor do the new overarching terms consider gradations in the increasing "abstraction" of higher levels of symbolic representation, a tendency towards schematic parsimony seen in the arts, and especially important in conceptual thought and mathematics. Differentiating various grades of presentation and *re*-presentation better traces the evolution of memory systems via feedback loops from kinetic/visual forms of iconic-imagery that likely expanded the human cortex to the tight condensations and abstractions of cognized symbolic signs—whether in word, object, or image.

Several distinctions along evolutionary/developmental lines need to be made: beginning at less-differentiated stages of our *presentational* function, eidetic imagery accentuates a visual record, then moves to more differentiated *re*-presentations. This progression illustrates that we start by "picturing" what we see, then move to higher abstracted forms, "representing" what we *know*. Distinguishing these phases of *re*-presentation traces an evolutionary progression moving from sensorimotor kinetic/*visual* input to more conceptual *re*-presentations filtered through signs which, in turn, reflect the cognitive status and mental development of different stages of hominid evolution via their products. These distinctions also highlight evolving memory systems and layering of more distinct gestural/linguistic signifiers over natural expressions. The importance of expanding memory systems linked to affective-experience cannot be overstressed. This is why, in my opinion, the role of innate emotional-expressions and imitative learning play such key roles in developing hominid representational capacities and also why they are phylogenetically secured.

Recent research (Solms, 2020) has shown that innate affect-expressions are triggered by stimuli *even when only partial or even no cortex* is present although these are probably not actually *felt*. Primal involuntary affect-expressions originate in the reticular activating system's periaqueductal gray (PAG) brainstem, an area that plays a major role in integrating behavioral responses to internal or external stressors. They are so well preserved in phylogenetically older brain regions because they signal instantly what is going on inside the organism. More subtly nuanced emotions, colored by cultural custom, develop later. From the get go, facial expression-recognition would have laid down a neural *template* predisposing our perceptual slant toward reading *meaning* into iconic form. I further believe that it is from these primal facial configurations, involving natural-expressive cries, that more articulate sound-calls, together with gestural components, lead eventually to syllabic-words.

Every animal leaves traces of what it was; man alone leaves traces of what he created.

—*J. Bronowski, 1973, p. 38*

Roughly 40,000 years ago a spectacular explosion in culture left us stone, clay carvings, and masterful art painted deep inside dark cave walls. We surmise that these were poorly illuminated, executed in uncomfortable positions that nevertheless took advantage of the natural uneven cave surface. In looking at these impressive images, we not only marvel at the artistic skill and their extraordinary beauty but note their precise verisimilitude reproduction, perfectly proportioned, and strangely affecting. We are moved by their immense evocative impact, conveying the speed of the charging bison herd, the thunderous roar of hooves, inviting us to identify with the tiny stick figures representing a group of hunters, understanding how exciting, exacting, and risky was their hunt for food and survival. (All children go through a predictable "stick figure" phase in drawing). What does this tell us of their minds? It tells us that our skilled ancient artists were still little-differentiated from their prey, their surround, and from each other in the group, and therefore were acutely attuned, operating with a *perceptual* memory-system producing *eidetic imagery*—the ability to call up and reproduce an exact facsimile of a percept still infused with the emotional impact of a *whole* situation. Signified *re*-presentations begin with condensations of perceptions, feelings, movement, and context, in sensorimotor processing of interconnected brainstem and mid-brain to higher cortical regions. No part of the brain is omitted in this process.

Prehistoric images project this condensation of ideo-kinetic, sensory-emotive identification with the objects they depict by a mind still merged with the situations of its environment so that the "picture" mirrors the endowments of that mind's undifferentiated stage of development. The great paleontologist Anati (2002a, 2002b) affirms, this through insightful interpretations of prehistoric art, reading into them a basic grammatical system of **"pictograms," "ideograms,"** and **"psychograms,"** the elemental

135

subject-sources expressing the early cognitive/emotive epistemological endowment of our species. One might say that these three, universal, foundational, signified-categories which, Anati explains, retain diagnostic value across different conditions and levels of cultural evolution, do so because they are templates for perceptual, cognitive, and emotional features of a language in which the *image is vocabulary*. Iconographic codes, here, depict not only major themes (sex, food, shelter), but also time-sequenced scenarios, exposing the analytic and allegorical conceptual models available to primitive mental organization. Like Freud in dreams, Anati finds in the prehistoric image a pictographic *cognition*, another *"mode of thought"* which leads to the requisite role of empathy, of *"felt-understanding,"* in the participant/observer's "interpretive stance."

Panovsky's (1962) iconographic analysis of levels of meaning and correlate interpretive requirements provide further insights into the minds of those who crafted these primal artistic expressions. With Freud (who likened psycho-analysis to surgery), Panovsky writes that trying to grasp the basic principles underlying subject, production, technical procedures, and presentation of image-*motifs,* calls on mental faculties akin to those of a "diagnostician" (p. 15)! The results, however, yield a three-tiered iconographic analysis of levels of meaning and requisite interpretive equipment. Our ancestral artists' *"primary* or *natural"* subject matter is depicted in ways that are "factual and expressional" fitting Panovky's first level. This requires an interpretative act that considers a *pre*-iconographic descriptive style, has some familiarity with the objects and events depicted, as well as the manner in which, under varying historical conditions, these "objects and events were conveyed by *forms"* (pp. 14–15). We are reminded of our recommended participant/observer stance for interpretations aimed at understanding all human meanings by resonating with the type/level of organization of their *forms*. The perceptual piece of early stages of internalization lead to a *presentational* form that *antecedes re-presentation* in psycho-iconographic terms. With *re-presentation* come subjective *meanings:* nowhere are these more palpable than in dreams.

We begin dreaming around the third year of life, and between ages five and twelve nightmares are common. The young nervous system is negotiating intense emotions with behavior, distinguishing between inside and outside, imagination and reality, wish and obtainable, while processing tons of information. Throughout life, most of this accommodating of impressions and experiences, past and present, and piecing them together, occurs in sleep. Along with first dreams comes a challenging early developmental hurdle. This "neuro-biological" differentiation process that took our ancestors millennia must now be accomplished by our contemporary eighteen-month-old toddler. Known as the first separation-individuation process (the second occurs in adolescence), and meticulously laid out stage by stage in M. Mahler's (*et all*, 1975) psychoanalytic empirical research, this phase is fraught with interpersonal drama and pitfalls. Once traversed successfully, however, it yields the inner image—evocative memory, and the psychologically imperative "object constancy," i.e., secure establishment of the "object" (person) in the mind's eye. Its consequential results for behavior-regulation, secure-attachments, cognition, and advances in linguistic-labelling are impressive. The precipitate of this momentous step for mind is a nascent *referential distance* in the use of signifiers. The "word" will slowly acquire new status as it moves inward to "inner speech" and eventually conceptual thought, as communication relies less on natural signals than on learned signs.

Dreams exhibit in *statu nascendi* how affects and drives are first *signified.* But dreams also have a developmental line: children's dreams show little or no "regression;" they are still fully embodied, their imagery clinging to the feelings that elicit them, whereas in adults a formal regression to this earlier mode of thinking is revived. When interpreting dreams, we unpack and trace meanings that are condensed into image-elements via profuse associations. Through this method we observe a representational sequence: from core felt-ideas > to emotion/drive into pictographs > from verbal narration > into > interpreted linguistic transcription. Each version is transcribed into a *completely different* semiotically represented *form.* Human cognition evolves via these *re*presentational means; what was unconscious becomes consciously *aware* when filtered through verbal signifiers.

The dream's composition reveals multi-sensorimotor, emotive, and linguistic cross-referenced source-points; presentational (figurative) *and* denotational (linguistic) semiotic-forms converge. Their *primary process* signifying mechanisms are precursors of linguistic tropes, the embodied fabric out of which all meanings in human cognition is represented and expressed. Through the interpretation of dreams, we witness the pre-, proto-, and semiotic sources and progressions of re-presentational steps. Moving through semiotic forms, the dream's experiential impact diminishes, away from intense emotions as it becomes *re*presented by conventional, conscious, signifiers.

The material of the dream's imagery, however, is constructed from "core ideas" which emerge from a "ready-made structure" (Freud, 1900, 445). They are reached only after unpacking many lead-associational threads. These core "ideas," then, are *there from the start!* And how could they not be? How else would we have survived without a core instinctual adaptive intelligence, neurally coded in accordance with principles of parsimony and energy preservation, propelling evolutionary advances continuously fortified by intense collaborative social groupings. I submit that these pre-formed ideas *are* the neural correlates of innate intelligence, *the essential kernels of human cognition condensed in a primary neural code.*

We have now moved seamlessly into the Cultural Code era and linguistic representation. The advent of speech marks a momentous event in human development; a shift from signifying *actions* to the use of a *symbolic medium*, so that "Between the clearest animal call of love or warning or anger, and man's least, trivial *word*, there lies a whole day of Creation... a whole chapter of evolution" (Langer, 1942, p. 103). The ability to speak our minds, this especially separates us from all other creatures. With words we *refer to* things, people, places, ideas, a whole new referential idiom through which to *filter* experience and thought: without words we have no instrument by which to name or orient ourselves in place and time; no medium to mediate impulse, or convey desires; no articulate means to determine intention, articulate ideas or concepts; no way of sequencing tasks, make plans, or narratize our stories. One word leads to another; causality is built in. Our minds develop under the imprinting stamps and sensory-impressions, the coded messages, and traditions, of *those* representational systems that dominate the society we grow up in. At first, our sensory-motor core receives these impressions. But gradually the whole is subsumed within the meta-coded linguistic vocabulary of our society. Language leads into a semantic that has been codified by convention in a culture; its lore's, beliefs, and expressive-gestural style, contain, encoded *within it,* the socio-cultural traditions, habits, and prejudices, of *that* place and time.

Eidetic memory dominates early presentational forms; here the *visual* record, tied to primitive affects and drives, produces a near-replica of the experience of the "thing" depicted: next, a more *subjective* stage is shaped by metonymy and metaphor—one thing *standing for another*, seeing the *familiar in the unfamiliar;* one might surmise that here "ignification" takes hold, belief is expressed through ritual and magic. As experience becomes increasingly filtered through a more precise system of syntactically aligned verbal-signs, language promotes the metacode of narrative, our *storying* mode. Each of these functional-forms of *representation* has its own organizational characteristics carried by different memory systems tied to different kinds of signified information. So, for example, a reflection or moral dilemma cannot be *represented abstractly* without language: alternate ways of expressing the same would have to be played out in actions or depicted through characters in a storyline. Overall mental organization, however, is contingent on *the developmental level at which a semiotic system is used, not on the semiotic medium itself.* The epigenesis of re-presentation illustrates how diverse modes of thought are the *manifest correlates* of a complex, layered, cerebral architecture of nested levels that develop greater efficiency via the use of semiotic vehicles. The developmental stages move from **presented**, to **re-presented**, to **referenced** signifiers, shifting away from sensory-motor embodied form towards mental abstraction.

In conclusion: I have examined the epigenesis of representation as it mirrors the evolution of the brain generating different levels and kinds of meanings in "gnosis"—*how* we know, tracing their ascendence from primordial origins to the nervous-system/brain of Sapiens, much as it is now. Representation engages the whole organism generating neural feedback-loops, modifying mnemonic/emotional centers, and altering the conveyance and interpretation of meanings by radically changing subjective experience, cognition, and behavioral means of expression. Representational capacities would have evolved gradually, with the cortex, interconnecting separate neocortical regions with subcortical, brainstem, and limbic areas, as these nuclei developed. If we now ask; "What are the conditions for "representability?" we can answer, a neocortex in a complex nervous system. Representation originates in seeds of mnemonic processes building on the internal image: this is our "mind's" instrument, what makes us the *"animal simbolicum."*

Via this inquiry, I have gone beneath Freud's *primary process,* through the dream's sources, into the neural circuitry manifest through their imagery. This reveals that the laws of abstraction emanate from, and are *already coded,* at neurological levels of organismic functioning, their iteration expressed through the increasing complexity of semiotic processes throughout evolutionary/developmental stages of our tree of re-presentation.

To be continued...

Lecture XII
Nature's Template
Sub specie aeternitatis

The human trajectory was prescribed in part by the initial molecular properties of heredity in life on earth.

—*C.J. Lumsden & E.O. Wilson, 1983, p. 55*

Any biological system that makes objects according to the rules of a code is generating biological artifacts, and a world of artifacts is fundamentally different form the world it came from.... There is the same logic, the same underlying principle behind the origin of life and the origin of mind. This is the code model of mind, the idea that there was a neural code at the origin of mind as there was a genetic code at the origin of life.

—*Barbieri, 2011, p. 380*

Abstract

This is the summation of previous talks on the evolutionary material I've presented. The three Barbierian macroevolutionary stages are revisited with an eye to tracing the course of two basic mechanisms, "copy and code," theoretical pillars in this model for the natural history of semiosis. Each of my prior talks moved through these three code-prompted stages from organic to neural to cultural sign-symbol systems, contributing the singular psychoanalytic piece through Freudian dream theory, without which the leap from body/brain to *mind* could not be fully clarified or comprehended.

The main question now is; if the two key mechanisms—copy and code—proposed as formulaic for all coding processes that (1) begin the promulgation of life and (2) self-propel semiotic progressions, in micro-developmental steps and macro-evolutionary stages, then we ought to be able to find them iterated and reiterated in different ways, isomorphically, at ever higher, more complex levels of organization of the human nervous system.

And the principal idea behind my conclusion is to demonstrate how, and in what ways, this is so.

* * * *

The discovery of the genetic code, set in motion a series of theoretical shock waves affecting various scientific communities leaving mainstream biology's basic chemistry-based theory more or less untouched. Among those who considered the consequences of finding coding and information-replication processes at the heart of the cells of life, M. Barbieri (1985) called for a new paradigm to accommodate its implications, proposing a semantic theory centering on the ribotype, the codemaker of the genetic code. His 1985 *Semantic Theory* contained two foundational principles: 1. that the cell is a trinity of genotype-phenotype-ribotype; and, 2. that evolution takes place by natural selection *and* natural conventions. From these ideas emerge two basic mechanisms on which Barbieri's theory centers—copy and code. Many new organic codes have since come to light, and he encourages biology to incorporate these basic processes into the biology of the future.

There followed many papers subsumed in a seminal book, *Code Biology* (Barbieri, 2015), elaborating his code-based evolutionary theory, leading to the establishment of a society and research community by the same name. Present at the origination of the interdisciplinary field of Biosemiotics, were it not for a core theoretical rift, Barbieri's *Code Biology* framework would be the founding backbone of these poly-disciplinary studies as an integral part of a unified community. Barbieri's exhaustive output and extensive expertise is grounded in detailed mastery over a wide range of related topics, his conceptual analysis, reaching well beyond the biological establishment, pointing to microcellular origins and evolution. The framework he devised regards biological sequencing as organic information, the micro-processes essential to life, and biological coding rules as *fundamental* observables. (Barbieri 2015, 34). His overall conceptual view is summarized in the following succinct passage:

142

...there are two distinct processes at the basis of life: the *copying* of genes and the *coding* of proteins. Genes are manufactured by molecular machines that can be referred to as *copymakers* and proteins by molecular machines that can be called *codemakers*. Copying and coding,... are both artifact-making processes and life as we know it requires both of them. We can truly say, therefore, that life is *artifact-making,* or, more precisely, that *life is artifact-making by copying and coding.*

—Barbieri, 2015, p. 12

Citing Crick's (1958) re-proposal of the Central Dogma of molecular biology, Barbieri (2015) writes: *DNA makes RNA (transcription) and RNA makes proteins (translation)* adding, *"the ribosome is decoder of genetic information"* (paraphrased from p. 37). Barbieri's main point is that organic codes show a way forward, his model resting on two key mechanisms underlying organic codes: "transcription and translation," copying and coding. Barbieri's *code theory of mind* is based on the idea that "mind is produced by a manufacturing process based on a neural code as proteins are produced by a manufacturing process based on the genetic code" (Barbieri, 2015, 111). A parallel drawn, the challenge now is to find and demonstrate its iterations.

Neither by training nor temperament can I venture into details of microbiology. I can, however, grasp broad principles and conceptualize their generalization within the overarching framework of three macro-evolutionary stages in the natural history of signification: organic, neural and cultural. If the copy-and-code formula at the micro-level in Barbieri's model is to serve as a template for the propulsion of evolution, then its transcribe-and-translate pattern must be iterated and reiterated isomorphically at ever higher levels of organization of the human nervous system. And this progression must be traceable through transition-phases and stable-stages via whatever manifest processes and expressions are observable, as these inform those advancements, both anatomical and socio-cultural, that would have generated significant evolutionary shifts. My goal here is to chart these progressions that uncover consistent bio-mechanisms underlying a continuous thread from molecular processes to the highest forms of cognitive abstraction, identifying how this template reiterates up a hierarchy of semiotic complexity.

First, nature certainly devised a most efficient, concise, energy-conserving means of encapsulating and transmitting information, and second; given the singular anatomical architecture of the human brain only our species can express the unique cognitive/semiotic capacities creating minds that feel and "think." In prior talks on the evolutionary course of semiosis, I chose what I consider to be crucial topics for the study of its origins, development, and cultural flowering. I took the analysis of *form* advocated by B. Russell (1953) as my approach because *signification,* like all organic/living things, generates its own morphological transformations, a development marked by organizational changes in functional *form.* Here, I summarize the essential points from my multidisciplinary-explorations, ending with a unifying hypothesis.

Re-presentation is the mark of a brain that can *"call things to mind."* This human ability to leap from body-to-mind, I suggest, originated in the embodied manifestation of organic gut-feelings as these evolved into overt physio/facial expressions. The connection from enteric nervous system to brain via the vagus nerve would have generated visible/audible expressions of inner states, an adaptive necessity arising from attachment and social-bonding needs. The resulting reciprocal visual/felt *re*-cognition would have laid neural foundations for physiognomic/imagistic ideation, reinforcing memory and internalized-learning via the mirror-neuron circuitry.

But why, you may ask, is this so interesting and important for psychoanalysis? Because the roots of psycho-analysis are deeply biological: we cannot avoid recognizing that the *brain* is the organ of mind. How hominid brains grew, and semiotic processes evolved, are tightly correlated with how *minds* developed. For Freud, the biological *was* the "bedrock" for the psychical (1937, p. 252). A research biologist and medical neurologist before establishing the psychoanalytic method, he insistently integrated body with psyche, his theories all embedded in evolutionary ideas. Nowhere was he more convinced of this connection than in his theory of dreams which, he believed, would reveal the early origins and prehistory of human *mental development.* As someone studying dreams from a meta-biosemiotic perspective, seeking continuity between soma and psyche along phylo- and onto-genetic lines, a bedrock coding template provides an appealing avenue to finding that continuity.

Of particular relevance in the transition from organic to *mental* (neural) processing, then, is the dream, a manifest-phenomenon bridging biological

---

and psychical processes, exhaustively analyzed along all dimensions by Freud (1900) who decoded its signifying meaning-making vocabulary. Accordingly, I operate on the assumption that copy-and-coding mechanisms at neural/mental levels work-through the human nervous system processing experiences by producing images that coagulate in the confluence of sensory-motor, perceptual, emotive, and mnemonic systems. Sensory-input feeds into the multidetermined subjective *form*ulations of dream-imagery: dreams are pictured thoughts. The templates of nature, copying-and-coding, or "code-poesis" in Barbieri's paradigm, I propose, very much apply to the dream which provides a window into this pivotal transition from organic to neural processing.

Freud's (1900) analysis of dreams lays out a two-tiered structure, manifest and latent: "The dream-thoughts and dream-content are . . . like two versions of the same subject-matter in two different languages, the dream-content seems like a transcript of the dream thoughts into another mode of expression" (1900, p. 277). Confusing manifest content with latent ideas means *missing the entire process of the "dream-work,"* a process that gives "things a new form" (p. 507). Looking closely, we find that the manifest dream is not merely a "pictured" *signifier for what it signifies*—and, hence, *a semiotic product* (a true "artifact" in Barbieri's language) but that this "labor of mind" is a *metaphorizing* process permeating *all* human cognition.

The *"dream-work,"* as Freud put it, *transcribes* the associational threads that went into the core "ideas," so that registrations of entire situations, often subliminal, are "copied" and "coded" as *signifiers* to compose sense-imagery that *represents* the core "ideas." Given the dream's formal regression, the "fabric of the dream thoughts" is "resolved into its raw material" (1900, p. 543). So, latent core "ideas" are transposed into imagery from a neural cluster akin to Luria's (1973) *"multidimensional"* (p. 284) or Damasios's (1999) *"convergence zones"* (p. 219) as a *"ready-made structure"* (Freud, 1900, p. 445) a "neural code." Luria (1973) elaborates: "the systems of connections into which traces of information reaching the subject are *coded with respect to different signs,* and consequently they form *multidimensional matrices* from which the subject must choose . . . the system which, at that particular moment, will form the basis for coding" (*original italics,* p. 284). Dream imagery expresses *these* choices.

The analytic interpretation of dreams highlights the proto-semiotic sources and progressions of *re*-presentational steps through various semiotic forms. Slowly, as the interpretive breakdown of the dream's imagery leads to its *core ideas*, the unconscious "thing-presentation" (Freud, 1915) is *transcribed* into the *thing-plus* the "word-presentation" (pp. 201–202). The copy-and-code formula is evident here in the mnemonic *"copying"* of perceptual input and *"coding"* its condensed *meanings* into iconic-form. Evident also are processes of internalization and re-externalization here projected onto the proscenium of mind. We surmise that artistic products inspired by personal insight issue from the same source.

Feelings, then, produce *meanings* manifest by mind in imagery, an eidetic-cognition that likely preceded articulate language as we know it. Since all memories are a *composite* of visual and sensory-motor emotional experiences in interactions *within* particular situations, dreams are sensory-emotive storied-situations, composed from memory-fragments triggered by, and mixed with, current impressions coded accorded to subjective import. However, the mental-image (and this applies also to visual-art) conveys laws of *conceptualization* rather than perception-proper a point that validates Freud's insistence on the *ideational essence* of dreams. This implies that dreams are *ideas without words* and that cognition is not contingent *on,* but only channeled *through,* the linguistic prism. Moreover, figurative symbols are inadequately represented by language: linear thought may be governed by linguistic form but intuitive sentience is not; it can be pictured, mimed, danced, sung, or dramatized. This is also why paleo-anthropologist Anati (2002, p. 68) can diagnose levels of cognitive development and interpret predominant themes of concern via iconographic content and form.

The parallel Barbieri draws between microprocess and mind is formed at the neural level, and the dream is its prototype. The image, in fact, is the nearest form for abstracting concepts. Mind emerges in metaphoric processes of *transcribing* sensori-input and *translating* this into subjective meanings, illustrating how neural-processing *cognizes by transcribing senses into imagery* depicting the material of ideas. The dream is the *in vivo* product of this confluence of perception, emotion, memory and meaning, a neural shift from sensorimotor experience to mental-representation that entails advances in various cerebral systems creating an *organizational rearrangement* (a morphological change in form).

But there is more here than meets the eye: consider this remarkable statement regarding *judgement* in dreams which, Freud (1900) states, does not belong to the "dream-work" but *"to the material of the dream-*

thoughts... having been lifted from them into the manifest content... as a ready-made structure" (original italics, p. 445). This would mean that our assessment and judgment, functions usually associated with *the cortex,* actually exist *prior* to any re-presentation, *already sentient* in a basic instinctive intelligence akin to "intuition," our gut feeling. It seems that the neurally coded "ideas," *inchoate as they may be,* condensed in a *"ready-made structure,"* require *formulation* (transcription) and re-coding (translation) via *a re-presentational medium* to come into view and be interpreted via semiotic vehicles explicit enough to become conscious.

This third level of *transcription* and *translation* occurs in the verbal interpretation of dreams, accomplished via language, our cultural code and primary instrument of communication and conscious thought. As the associational threads and meanings encased in each image-element are unpacked, we *transcribe* image into words, *translating* their meanings into conventional linguistic terms. The end-result is a return to the core *ideas, or concepts,* now *referred* to linguistically. In fact, all semiotic systems seem to begin in tight "abstractions," unfold via various stages of *representational re-organization,* and end up again expressing high abstractions: we see this in iconography, mathematics, alphabets, thought, the story-paradigm, and its apotheosis in the digital algorithm, and A.I., our closest imitation yet of the human mind.

What I observe is an *abstractive instinct,* a tendency built into our "coding" biology, in tight, efficient, information-containing-and-transmitting processes observable across biological systems, including those that hook onto a semiotic instrument. This predisposition for semiotic efficiency and development, I stress, is *already* there in humans, innate and, in fact, predisposed towards formulation through diverse media. And although language is indeed the basis for "all conceptual systems" (Feldman, 2008, 95) it merely enhances, embellishes, and conveys thoughts, expanding mental acumen through explicit communication and articulate thought.

The importance of Freud's theory of *The Interpretation of Dreams* is this: it presents a microcosm of several key transitions; first, an organic *transmission* whereby sensory-emotive input merges with mnemonic-processes in neural coding; then a tran*scription from emotional feelings into mental imagery* by a "primary-process" mode of thought; and then, from iconic-expressive *re*presentations to an interpretive linguistic *translation* into a "secondary-process" mode of thought. I think it significant that this same trajectory is repeated in the history of writing. These transformations—the first an organic transmission of feelings, the second a transposition into sensory-emotive imagery, the third an interpretive translation into linguistic form—*illustrate a semiotic sequence from organic to neural to cultural coding processes that, I submit, recapitulates our evolutionary development in the use of signs, and corresponds to Barbieri's code model in tracing the natural history of semiosis.*

The importance of memory, mirroring, mimicry, and social coding, in all of this cannot be overstressed. This is why I believe emotional-expressions and imitative learning play such key roles in developing human re-presentation capacities, and why they are phylogenetically secured. Progress from innate signals to oro-gestural sign use (Rizzini, 2015, 2018) resulting from mirroring and mimicking behaviors in family/group life, puts *imitative learning*—copying and coding (assigning meaning and fixing in memory)—at the *forefront of all early development.* The mirror neurons are not only heavily at play in kinetic imitation, but recent research finds this circuitry implicated in conceptual-thought as well (Gallese & Lackoff, 2005; Cuccio & Gallese, 2018). This makes perfect sense considering Freud's analysis of dream construction where "ideas," invisible as they may be before their representation, are, in fact, the starting-point and source of dreams.

As we move through various early developmental stages, we rapidly begin to filter experience and modulate behavior through learned culture-specific sign-systems, articulating meanings through more explicit verbal vehicles of semiotic mediation. Learning and accommodation graft prior forms of experience and knowledge onto what is newly learned so that a sensorimotor-core and metaphoric-processing remain at the heart of all cognition. But the crucial functions of the mirror-neuron circuitry early on in imitation and internalization leave indelible dynamic-schemas of relationships, entire scenarios of interactions, and their echo, in language.

The biological blueprint of our genetically-coded language centers oblige us to take an embodied view of linguistic-origins as evolving out of behavioral roots in our phylogenetically-secured primary signaling-system; emotional expressions. Language emerges out of this soil of expressive-communicative behaviors that begin in natural-signals quickly molding into oro-gestural (Rizzini, 2015, 2018) indicative sounds, to flower into curated denotive verbal-signifiers. This makes language not only a cultural "artifact" (in the Barbierian sense) transmitted by convention, but a prime example of the evolutionary feedback between socio-cultural input and organic-cerebral evolution. Once again, I emphasize the mirror neurons, just below language centers in the left hemisphere, because they produce the *copy-and-code template* for new learning. Sensory-input is mimicked, *copied*, internalized, *transcribed* and *coded* according to subjective import and custom. Nowhere in our socio-cultural evolution is the copy-and-code formula so clearly illustrated as in language.

Beginning early, infants emit a single, simple, sound—two vowels/two consonants—and the world has changed! parent and child meet in the tacit understanding that this sound *means* something! Ah, the "name"! *Everything* is in a name—the "thing," object, place, or person, is soon held in the mind's eye and an empowered toddler will now declare "desire" verbally! Into the "word" flow a flood of sensory-emotive associations only slowly to recede, leaving an abstract sign. Single words cluster into two, three, and several-word phrases: linguistic communications radically modify the quality of interactions just as grammar and syntactical sequencing, by their very nature, transform the quality of thought. The pronoun "I" (a late arrival in evolution according to Jaynes, 1976) will distinguish the self from all else to state intent, tell tales, and declare what is NOT wanted with the strident No! We grow acculturated internalizing local tone and custom: the private goes under as the social façade takes shape. More even than place, taste, or topography, the mother "tongue" plants the deepest roots at the center of identity. It will be quite some time, however, before the sign-system of words and language-in-communication achieve their full symbolic impact on the development of thought. The most important consequence of language fluency on human cognition is that by its denotive objectification and increasingly symbolic character, it creates acts of *reference* over mere *representation.* The far-reaching effect of this is further distancing from the "thing" itself and a commensurate increase in abstract-thought afforded by semiotic instruments. We see this historically in developments in art and the evolution of beliefs, rituals, reasoning, and religion.

In conclusion: This summary supports the Barbierian code-based evolutionary framework in finding consistent bi-directional impact in interactive feedback-loops between socio-cultural advancements and the development of human cerebral capacities. At first, these propel the evolutionary expansion of the brain itself and subsequently the *reorganization* of existing units, especially cortical functions.

The seeds of life contain a vital template, not an *élan vital,* but an inherent generative process with formulative and transmissive properties. This patterned copy-and-code template recurs in many biological systems at all levels in isomorphic configurations, physically and mentally. In a short communication R. Langs (2014), similarly, found evidence of what he called an "archetypal mental coding process," an "organizing force in nature that cuts across adaptation... at microscopic and macroscopic levels" (p. 6).

The story of the natural history of semiosis is embedded in this copy-and-code formula beginning at the start and of life, evolving up a hierarchy of complexity through the human nervous system and brain. Reaching the neural level, this template underlies all forms of new learning and accommodation, engaging all sensory-motor, emotive, and mnemonic processes connecting body and mind, producing imagery that is observable at the juncture of the dream's elements. It is deeply gratifying to confirm Freud's (1900) conviction that the dream's pictographic signifying processes reveal an earlier "mode of thought," and that using his method and analysis effectively reaffirms continuity between body and mind. The coded "idea" is, in fact, the starting point of human cognition, whereupon its *signifying* modes unfold, projected into various forms of sign re-presentation.

My goal here has been to uncover the reiteration of those bio-mechanisms underlying a continuous thread, from molecular processes to the highest forms of cognitive abstraction, to identify how this template reiterates semiotically, up a hierarchy of complexity, in the evolutionary history of semiosis. Barbieri's model takes us up to the third macroevolutionary stage. But are we not already well into a fourth stage? Digitally governed, contrived by the algorithm (Aragno, 2023), and realized through computers, we are rapidly being overrun by AI and robotic externalizations of many human functions, a "mind" of a virtual age, which I have labeled the Computational Era.

To be continued... ...

Postscript

"...five hundred years of humanism may be coming to an end as humanism transforms itself into something we must helplessly call posthumanism."
—*I. Habib, 1977, p. 212*

The dream runs through this series as starting and end point. Its thematic undertones in human codes, deciphered and constructed, converged once my focus shifted towards our mental prehistory, leading into our current time. But its source remains the Freudian analysis of dreams. The overarching sweep, then, is over the course of just one century: how psychoanalysis began, and, perhaps, how humanism is ending, ideas that bookend this work.

Certainly, the tectonic plates of human existence are shifting, paradigms are crumbling, daily life is changing, impacting how we communicate, think, and relate. Reading, writing, even articulate language, are all in decline as becoming computer and cellphone adept have taken over. Is humanism dying as Habib predicted, and is the cause our addiction and dependence on screens? Nothing as yet is clear except that there has never been such rapid or radical a change in human mentation. These talks and my exploration will continue, as long as energy and age permit, but this seems like the right place to end this work.

It is deeply gratifying to confirm Freud's (1900) conviction that the dream's pictographic processes reveal an earlier 'mode of thought:' by examining his method we encounter the way body is continuous with mind. It is equally rewarding to find concordance between Barbieri's neural code model of brain/mind and Freud's observations of dream structure, over one hundred years ago. The coded 'idea' is, in fact, the starting point of human cognition whereupon *signifying* modes unfold, projecting *ideas* through various forms of sign re-presentation.

151

I hope that in this 'integration' I have contributed to the march towards new knowledge realizing what several great minds, each in their own way, advocated, namely; the rapprochement between the sciences and humanities in unifying knowledge through rigorous interdisciplinarity. S. Freud, wove Darwinian drives into a deep exploration of the human soul; B. Russell's logical philosophy in science foresaw the importance of the understanding of general forms; E.O. Wilson's new naturalism integrated anthropology with animal/human behavior and prehistory in Sociobiology; and M. Barbieri, who, observing the presence of coding throughout life-systems introduced semiotic processes into biology and evolution. It is quite possible that for now this conceptual framework has come closest to the aspirations expressed below:

"The theory of human nature that prevails in the end will be the one that aligns social behavior and history with all that is known about human biology. It will correctly and uniquely characterize the known operations of the human mind and the patterns of cultural diversity. At issue are the very limits of the natural sciences."
—*C.J. Lumsden and E.O. Wilson 1983, p. 85*

To be continued.....
New York City, 2025

Bibiliography

This bibliography lists the body of readings undergirding these talks. However, because these lectures present my own integration and synthesis, much material from the psychoanalytic literature that is inherent is not listed. Where a specific idea is taken, name and date are attributed.

Ackoff, R. L. (1975). *Redesigning the Future*. New York: John Wiley.

Almaky, M. (2020). Quantum Biosemiotics: From Numerous Interpretations to Semiosis Simultaneous Interpretations. Draft presentation for an international conference at the University of Bucharest.

Anati, Emmanuel (2002a). La Struttura Elementare dell'Arte. *Centro Camuno di Studi Preistorici*. 22. Valcamonica, IT: Edizione del Centro.

———— (2002b). Lo Stile come Fattore Diagnostico nell'Arte Preistorica. *Studi Camuni*. 23. Valcamonica, IT: Edizione del Centro.

Aragno, A. (1997/2016) *Symbolization: Proposing A Developmental Paradigm for a New Psychoanalytic General Theory of Mind*. New York: IPBooks.

———— (2005). Book Review: *The First Idea: How Symbols, Language, and Intelligence Evolved from our Primate Ancestors to Modern Humans*. S.I. Greenspan & S.G. Shanker, DaCapo Press 2005. *The Psychoanalytic Quarterly* 74:1154–1164.

———— (2008/1016). *Forms of Knowledge: A Psychoanalytic Study of Human Communication*. New York: IPBooks.

———— (2008). The Language of Empathy: An Analysis of its Constitution, Development, and Role in Psychoanalytic Listening. *Journal of the American Psychoanalytic Association* 56:713–740.

———— (2022). A Revised Psychoanalytic Model of Mind and Communication in Body-Mind Continuity. In *Psychoanalysis and the Mind-Body Problem*, ed., J. Mills. London: Routledge, pp. 204–226.

———— (2023). The Algorithm: Mind of a Virtual Era. Our Code of Codes. *International Journal of Psychoanalysis and Education: Subject, Action, and Society.* 3(2):1–22.

———— (2025). Code Poiesis: Life's Fuel. *BioSystems, 252:105& Co.460,* June Special Issue doi: *https://doi.org/10.1016/j.biosystems.2025.105460*

Augustine of Hippo (389 AD). *De Doctrina Christiana.* In *Sancti Augustini Opera,* 1963, ed. W.M. Green. Vienna: CSEL 8.

Bakhtin, M. M. (1981).*The Dialogic Imagination,* Ed. M. Holquist. Austin: University of Texas Press.

————— (1986). *Speech Genres and Other Late Essays,* ed. Caryl Emerson & Michael Holquist, trans. V. W. McGee. Austin: University of Texas Press.

Barbieri, M. (1985). *The Semantic Theory of Biology.* New York: Routledge.

———— (2006a). Semantic Biology and the Mind-Body Problem: The Theory of the Conventional Mind. *Biological Theory* 1(4):352–356.

———— (2006b). Life and semiosis: The real nature of Information and Meaning. *Semiotica,* 158(1/4):233–254.

———— (2008). The Code Model of Semiosis: The First Steps Towards a Scientific Biosemiotics. *The American Journal of Semiotics* 24(1/3):23–37.

———— (2009). Three Types of Semiosis. *Biosemiotics.* 2(1):19–30.

———— (2010). On the Origin of Language. *Biosemiotics* 3(2):201–223.

———— (2011). Origin and Evolution of the Brain. *Biosemiotics* 4(3):369–399.

———— (2012). Codepoiesis—the Deep Logic of Life. *Biosemiotics* 5(3):297–299.

———— (2012). Code Biology—A New Science of Life. *Biosemiotics* 5(3):411–437.

———— (2013). Letter to the Editor. November 17th, 2013. Online January 3, 2014, *Biological Theory.*

———— (2014). From Biosemiotics to Code Biology. *Biological Theory,* 9(2):239–249.

———— (2015). *Code Biology. A New Science of Life.* New York: Springer.

———— (2016). A New Theory of Development: The Generation of Complexity in Ontogenesis. *Philosophical Transaction of the Royal Society A.*

———— (2018). What is Code Biology? *BioSystems* 164:1–10.

———— (2020a). The Semantic Theory of Language. *BioSystems,* 190:104100.

———— (2020b). A Bird's-Eye View. *Gatherings in Biosemiotic, volume XX.* Tartu: University of Tartu Press, pp. 72–91.

Bateson, G. (1972). *Steps to an Ecology of Mind.* New York: Ballantine.

———— (1979). *Mind and Nature: A Necessary Unity.* New York: Dutton.

Bible, *King James, New International Bible.*

Berlinski, D. (2000). *The Advent of the Algorithm.* San Diego, New York, London: Harcourt, Inc.

Bronowski, J. (1973). *The Ascent of Man*, Boston, Toronto: Little Brown & Co.

Bruner, J. (1983). *Child's Talk: Learning to Use Language*, New York: W. W. Norton & Co.

———— (1990). *Acts of Meaning.* Cambridge, MA: Harvard University Press.

Calvin, W.H. (1996). *How Brain's Think. Evolving Intelligence, Then and Now.* New York: Basic Books.

———— (1998), *The Cerebral Code. Thinking a Thought in the Mosaic of the Mind.* Cambridge, MA: The MIT Press.

Carr, N. (2011). *The Shallows: What the Internet is Doing to Our Brains.* New York: W.W. Norton & Co., 2020.

Charlesworth, B&D (2017). *Evolution. A Very Short Introduction.* Oxford: Oxford University Press.

Cobley, P. Ed (2010). *The Routledge Companion to Semiotics*, New York: Routledge.

Crick, F.H.C. (1958). On Protein Synthesis: Symp. *Soc. Exp Biol 12*:138–163.

Cuccio, V. & Gallese, V. (2018). A Piercean account of concepts: grounding abstraction in phylogeny through a comparative neuroscientific perspective. *Philosophical Transaction Brstb.royalsocietypublishing.org*

Davis, L.K. & Panksepp, J. (2018). *The Emotional Foundations of Personality. A Neurobiological and Evolutionary Approach.* New York: W.W. Norton & Co.

Damasio, A. (1994). *Descartes's Error; Emotion, Reason, and the Human Brain.* New York: Harper-Collins.

———— (1999). *The Feeling of What Happens; Body and Emotion in the making of Consciousness,* New York: Harcourt.

———— 2003). *Looking for Spinoza; Joy, Sorrow, and the Feeling Brain.* New York: Harcourt.

———— (2010). *Self Comes to Mind. Constructing the Conscious Brain.* New York: Vintage Books.

———— (2018). *The Strange Order of Things. Life, Feelings and the Making of Cultures.* New York: Vintage Books.

Darwin, C. (1872). *The Expression of the Emotions in Man and Animals,* London: Penguin Classics, 2009.

———— (1871). *The Descent of Man, and Selection in Relation to Sex.* Princeton: Princeton University Press, 1981.

Beacon, T. (1997). *The Symbolic Species: Co-evolution of Language and the Human Brain* London: Penguin Books.

Dehaene, S. (2014). *Consciousness and the Brain; Deciphering how the Brain codes our Thoughts.* New York: Penguin Books.

De Waal, F. (1996). *Good Natured. The Origins of Right and Wrong in Humans and Other Animals* Cambridge, MA: Harvard University Press.

Domingos, P. (2015). *The Master Algorithm: How the Quest for the Ultimate Learner Machine Will Remake our World.* New York: Basic Books.

Eccles, J.C. (1989)., *Evolution of the Brain: Creation of the Self.* London: Routledge,

Edds, M.V. Jr., Editor-in-Chief (1969). *Communication in Development* Proceedings of the 28th Symposium, The Society for Developmental Biology, Boulder, CO, June 16–18, 1969. Cambridge, MA: Academic Press.

Edelson, M. (1975). *Language and Interpretation in Psychoanalysis.* Chicago: The University of Chicago Press.

Edelman, M.G. (1992). *Bright Air, Brilliant Fire: On the Matter of Mind.* New York: Basic Books.

Ekman, P. (1980). *The Face of Man: Expression of Universal Emotions in New Guinean Village.* New York: Garland STPM Press.

———— ed. (2006). *Darwin and Facial Expression. A century of Research in Review.* San Jose, CA: Malor Books.

———— & Freisen, W.V. (1969). The Repertoire of Non-Verbal Behavior: Categories, Origins, Usage and Coding. *Semiotica* 1:49–98.

———— & Oster, H. (1979). Facial Expression of Emotion. *Annual Review of Psychology* 30:527–555.

Ellis, G. & Solms, M. (2018). *Beyond Evolutionary Psychology. How and Why Neuropsychological Modules Arise.* Cambridge, UK: Cambridge University Press.

Emmeche, C. (2004). *Causal Processes, Semiosis, and Consciousness, in Crossdisciplinary Studies in Dynamic Categories,* ed. J. Seibit. Dordrecht: Kluwen.

———— (1972). *Emotions in the Human Face.* San Jose. CA: Malor Books.

Fauconnier, G. & Turner, M. (2002). *The Way We Think: Conceptual Blending and the Mind's Hidden Complexities.* New York: Basic Books.

Favareau, D. (2010). *Essential Readings in Biosemiotics.* Heidelberg: Springer-Science.

———— (2015). Symbols are Grounded not in Things but in Scaffolding Relations and their Semiotic Constraints (Or How the Referential Generality of Symbol Scaffolding Governs Minds.). *Biosemiotics, 8:235–255.*

Feldman, A.J. (2008). *From Molecule to Metaphor. A Neural Theory of Language.* Cambridge, MA: MIT Press.

Erdelyi, M.H. (1985*). Psychoanalysis: Freud's Cognitive Psychology.* New York. W.H. Freeman & Company.

Finn, E. (2017). *What do Algorithms Want: Imagination in the Age of Computing.* Cambridge, MA: The MIT Press.

Freud, S. (1895). Project for a Scientific Psychology. *Standard Edition* 1:295–391.

Frege, G. (1892). *On Sense and Reference [Über Sinn und Bedeutun*g], Zeitschrift für Philosophie und philosophische Kritik, 100:25–50.

———— (1900). *The Interpretation of Dreams,* Part I, *Standard Edition* 4.

———— (1900). *The Interpretation of Dreams,* Part II, *Standard Edition* 5.

———— (1915a). The Unconscious, in Papers on Metapsychology. *Standard Edition* 14:161–215.

———— (1915b). The Unconscious, Appendix B: Psycho-Physical Parallelism *in Papers on Metapsychology Standard Edition* 14:206–208.

———— (1925). An Autobiographical Study. *Standard Edition* 10:3–70.

———— (1937). Analysis Terminable and Interminable, *Standard Edition* 23:209–254.

———— (1940). An Outline of Psychoanalysis. *Standard Edition* 23:139–208.

———— & Breuer, J. (1895). *Studies on Hysteria.* New York: Basic Books Classics, 2000.

Gallese, V. (2001). The "Shared manifold" Hypothesis: From Mirror Neurons to Empathy. *Journal of Consciousness Studies* 8(5–7):33–50.

———— (2003). The Roots of Empathy: The Shared Manifold Hypothesis and the Neural Basis of Intersubjectivity. *Psychopathology 36:171–180.*

———— (2007). Intentional Attunement: The Mirror Neuron System and its Role in Interpersonal Relations. (Unpublished Presentation). *Meeting of the Philoctetes Society,* NYC, Winter, 2007.

———— & Lakoff, G (2005). The Brain's Concepts: The Role of the Sensory-Motor System in Conceptual Knowledge. *Cognitive Neuropsychology* 22(3/4):455–479.

———— (2008). Mirror Neurons and the Social Nature of Language: The Neural Exploitation Hypothesis. *Social Neuroscience* 3(3–4).317–333.

Gardner, H. (1982). *Art, Mind and Brain,* New York: Basic Books.

Gazzaniga, M.S. (2018). *The Consciousness Instinct. Unravelling the Mysteries of How the Brain makes the Mind.* New York: Farrar, Strauss, & Giroux.

Goodman, N. (1984). *Of Mind and Other Matters.* Cambridge, MA: Harvard University Press.

Greenspan, S. & Shanker, S. (2004). *The First Idea: How Symbols, Language, and Intelligence Evolved from Our Primate Ancestors to Modern Humans.* Cambridge, MA: Da Capo Press.

Hanson, N. R. (1958). *Patterns of Discovery: An Inquiry into the Conceptual Foundations of Science.* London: Cambridge University Press.

Harari, Y. N. (2015). *Sapiens: A Brief History of Mankind.* New York: Harper-Collins.

———— (2019). *21 Lessons for the 21st Century.* New York: Penguin Random House.

Hassan, Ihab (1977). Prometheus as Performer: Towards a Posthuman Culture? In *Performance in Postmodern Culture,* eds. M. Benamou & C. Caramella. Madison, WI: Coda Press, p. 212.

Hawkes, J. (2003), How Has the Human Brain Evolved Over the Years? *Scientific American Mind* 24(3):76. doi:10.1038/scientificamericanmind0713-76b

Hayles, N. K. (1999). *How We Became Posthuman: Virtual Bodies in Cybernetics, Literature, and Informatics*. Chicago: University of Chicago Press.

Headrick, D. R. (2009). *Technology: A World History*. Oxford: Oxford University Press.

Hegel, G.W. F. (1807). Introduction. *Lectures on the History of Philosophy*, trans. T. M. Knox & A.V. Miller. Oxford: Oxford University Press, 1987.

Hoffmeyer, J. (1993). *Signs of Meaning in the Universe*. Bloomington: Indiana University Press.

Izard, C. E. (1968). The Emotions as a Culture-Common Framework of Motivational Experience and Communicative Cues. Report No-Nr-Tr30 to sponsoring agency Office of Naval of Naval Research, Washington, DC, July 1968.

———— (1971). *The Face of Emotion*. New York: Appleton Century-Croft.

———— (1977). *Human Emotions*. New York: Plenum Press.

James, W. (1890). *The Principles of Psychology*. In *Great Books of the World*, ed. R.M. Hutchins, Vol. 53.

Jaynes, J. (1976). *The Origins of Consciousness in the Breakdown of the Bicameral Mind*. Boston: Houghton Mifflin Co.

Johnson, M. (1987). *The Body in the Mind: Bodily Basis of Meaning, Imagination, and Reason*. Chicago; The University of Chicago Press.

———— (2007). *The Meaning of the Body: Aesthetics of Human Understanding*. Chicago: University of Chicago Press

Konner, M. (1982). *The Tangled Wing. Biological Constraints on the Human Spirit*. New York: Holt, Rinehart and Winston.

Kövecses, Z. (2003). *Metaphor and Emotion. Language, Culture, and Body in Human Feeling*. Cambridge: Cambridge University Press.

Kull, K. (2014). Towards a Theory of Evolution of Semiotic Systems. *Chinese Semiotic Studies* 10(3):485–495. doi 10.1515/cc2014-0039

Kuhn, T. S. (1962). *The Structure of Scientific Revolutions*. Chicago: University of Chicago Press.

Lakoff, G. & Johnson, M. (1980). *Metaphors We Live By*. Chicago: The University of Chicago Press.

Lane, H. (1976). *The Wild Boy of Aveyron.* Cambridge, MA: Harvard University Press.

Langer, S. K. (1942). *Philosophy in a New Key.* Cambridge, MA: Harvard University Press.

———— (1967). *Mind: An Essay on Human Feeling,* Vol. 1, Baltimore, MD: Johns Hopkins University Press.

———— (1972). *Mind: An Essay on Human Feeling,* Vol. II, Baltimore, MD: John Hopkins Universities Press.

———— (1982). *Mind: An Essay on Human Feeling,* Vol. III, Baltimore, MD: John Hopkins Universities Press.

Langs, R. (2014). An Archetypal Mental Coding Process. *Biosemiotics, Special Issue on Code Biology 7:299–307.*

Leary, T. (1984). Access Codes & Carnival Blasts. *High Frontiers* 1: 24.

———— (1992). From LSD to Virtual Reality. Lecture given at Sonoma State University, October 19, 1992.

Le Doux, J. (1996). *The Emotional Brain, The Mysterious Underpinnings of Emotional Life.* New York: Simon and Schuster.

———— (2019). *The Deep History of Ourselves; The Four-Billion-Year Story of How We Got Conscious Brains.* New York: Penguin Books.

Licklider, J.C.R. (1957). Toward a Man Machine System for Thinking, August 20, 1957, In *Licklider Papers.* MIT Libraries, Cambridge, MA.

Livingston, R.B. (1978). *Sensory Processing, Perception, and Behavior.* New York: Raven Press.

Loye, D. (1983). *The Sphinx and the Rainbow. Brain, Mind and Future Vision.* Boulder: Shambhala.

Lumsden, C.J. & Wilson, E.O. (1983*). Promethean Fire: Reflections on the Origins of Mind.* Cambridge, MA: Harvard University Press.

Luria, A.R. (1963). *Cognitive Development: Its Cultural and Social Foundations,* trans. M. Lopez-Morillas & L. Solotaroff, ed M. Cole. Cambridge, MA: Harvard University Press.

———— (1973). *The Working Brain.* New York: Basic Books.

MacLean, P.D. (1973). *The Triune Concept of the Brain and Behavior.* Toronto: University of Toronto Press.

Mahler, M.S., Pine, F., & Bergman, A. (1975). *The Psychological Birth of the Human Infant.* New York: Basic Books.

Marshack, A. (1972). *The Roots of Civilization.* New York: McGraw-Hill.

Masson, J.M. (1985). *The Complete Letters of Sigmund Freud to Wilhelm Fleiss, 1887–1904*. Cambridge: MA: Harvard University Press.

Maturana, H., & Varela, S.A. (1980). *Autopoieis and Cognition: The Realization of the Living*. Dordrecht: D. Riedl.

McCulloch, W. (1965). *Embodiment of Mind*. Cambridge, MA: MIT Press.

Mitchell, W.J.T., ed. (1980). *On Narrative*. Chicago: Chicago University Press.

Modell, A. (1997). Reflections on Metaphor and Affects. *Annual of Psychoanalysis 25:219–234.*

Ogden, C.K. & Richards, I.A. (1923). *The Meaning of Meaning*. Orlando: Harcourt Brace Janovich.

Olds, D.D. (2000). A Semiotic Model of Mind. *Journal of the American Psychoanalytic Association 48(2):497–529.*

Ott, B. & Domenico, M. (2015). Conceptualizing Meaning in Communication Studies. In *A Century of Communication Studies. The Unfinished Conversation,* eds. P.J. Gehrke & W. M. Keith. London: Routledge, pp. 234–260.

Panksepp, J. (1998). *Affective Neuroscience: The Foundations of Human and Animal Emotions.* London: Oxford University Press.

———— (2000). Emotions as Natural Kinds within the Mammalian Brain. In *Handbook of Emotions,* eds. M. Lewis & J. Haviland. New York: Guilford Press, pp. 87–107.

———— (2005). Affective Consciousness: Core Emotional Feelings in Animals and Humans. *Consciousness and Cognition* 14(1):30–80.

Panksepp, J. & Biven, L. (2012). *The Archeology of Mind; Neuroevolutionary Origins of Human Emotion.* New York: W.W. Norton & Co.

Panofsky, E. (1962). *Studies in Iconography: Humanistic Themes in the Art of the Renaissance.* New York: Harper & Row.

Patte, H. H. (1969). How Does a Molecule Become a Message? Presentation at *Communication in Development.* 28th Symposium, The Society for Developmental Biology, Boulder, CO, June 16–18, 1969, Editor-in-Chief, M. V. Edds, Jr. Cambridge, MA: Academic Press.

Penfield, W. & Perot, P. (1963). The Brain's Record of Visual and Auditory Experience. *Brain* 86(4): 596–694.

Penfield, W. (1975). *The Mystery of The Mind: A Critical Study of Consciousness in the Brain.* Princeton: Princeton University Press.

Piaget, J. (1970). *Genetic Epistemology.* New York: Columbia University Press.

———— & Inhelder, B. (1969). *The Psychology of the Child.* New York: Basic Books.

Plutchick, R., (1980a). *Emotions: A Psychoevolutionary Synthesis,* New York: Harper & Row.

———— (1984). "Emotions: A General Psychoevolutionary Theory," in *Approaches to Emotions,* eds. K. R. Scherer & P. Ekman. Hillsdale, NJ: Lawrence Erlbaum Associates, Inc.

———— & Kellerman, H. eds. (1980b). *Emotions: Theory, Research and Experience.* Cambridge, MA: Academic Press.

Read, H. (1955). *Image and Idea: The Function of Art in the Development of Human Consciousness.* Cambridge, MA: Harvard University Press.

Rid, T. (2016). *Rise of the Machines A Cybernetic History.* New York: W.W. Norton & Co.

Rizzini, T. (2015). *Come Imparammo a Parlare.* Rome: Aracne.

———— (2018). The Cultural Linguistic Code. *Journal of Life Sciences* 12:59–63. doi: 10.17265/1934-7391/2018.01.006

Rycroft, C. (1956). Symbolism and its relationship to the primary and secondary process. *International Journal of Psychoanalysis* 27:137–157.

———— (1958). An Enquiry into the Function of Words in the Psychoanalytic Situation *International Journal of Psychoanalysis* 39:408–415.

Ryle, G. (1949). *The Concept of Mind.* London: Hutchinson & Co. Publishers Ltd.

Rizzolati, G. Fogassi, L. & Gallese, V. (2001). Neurophysiological Mechanisms Underlying the Understanding and Imitation of Action. *Nature Neuroscience Reviews* 2:661–670.

Russell, B. (1953). On Scientific Method in Philosophy. In *Mysticism and Logic.* London: Penguin Books, pp. 95–119.

Shannon, C. (1948). A Mathematical Theory of Communication. *Bell Systems Technology Journal* 27:379–424 & 623–656.

Sharpe, E.F. (1937/1978). *Dream Analysis.* New York: Brunner/Mazel Publisher.

———— (1940). Psycho-Physical Problems Revealed in Language: An Examination of Metaphor. In *Collected Papers on Psycho-Analysis*: London: Hogarth Press, 1950, pp. 155–169.

Schmandt Besserat, D. (2019). Archeological Tokens. in *Tokens, Culture, Connections, Communities*, eds. A. Crisa, M. Gkikaki, & C. Rowan. Royal Numismatic Society, Special Publication 51:1–15.

Schwartz, J.M. & Begley, S. (2002). *The Mind and the Brain: Neuroplasticity and the Power of Mental Force.* New York: HarperCollins.

Snel, B. (1953). *The Discovery of the Mind: The Greek Origins of European Thought,* 2nd Ed, trans. T.G Rosenmeyer. New York: Angelico Press. 2013.

Solomon, M. (1998). *Beethoven,* 2nd Revised Ed. New York: Schirmer Books.

Solms, M. (2020). Online lecture April 18th.

———— (2021). Personal communications.

Stampe, D. (1968). Toward a Grammar of Meaning. *The Philosophical Review* 77(2):137–174.

Sulloway, F.J. (1979*). Freud: Biologist of the Mind.* New York: Basic Books.

Tarnas, R. (1991). *The Passion of the Western Mind: Understanding the Ideas that Have Shaped Our World View.* New York: Ballantine Books.

Tomasello, M. (2019). *Becoming Human. A Theory of Ontogeny.* Cambridge, MA: The Belknap Press, Harvard University Press.

Tomkins, S.S. (1962), *Affects, Imagery, Consciousness Vol.1-The Positve Affects.* New York: Springer.

———————— (1963), *Affects, Imagery, Consciousness Vol 2. The Negative Affects,* New York: Springer.

Van Wagner, A. (2020). *Is This the Most Interesting Idea in All of Science? Neurons Might Contain Something Incredible within Them.* Interview with Randy Gallistel, April 12, 2021.

Vygotsky, L. (1934). *Thinking and Speech: Psychological Investigations.* Moscow: Gosudarstvennoe Sotsialno-Ekonomicheskoe Izdatel'stvo.

———— (1962). *Thought and Language,* eds & trans. E. Hanfmann & G. Vakar. Cambridge, MA: MIT Press

———— (1977). *From the Notebooks of L.S. Vygotsky. Moscow University Record: Psychology* 2: 89–95.

——— (1978). *Mind in Society: The Development of Higher Psychological Processes*, ed. M. Cole, V. John-Steiner, S. Scribner, & E. Souberman. Cambridge, MA: Harvard University Press.

——— (1991). *Obras Escogidas.* Vol. 1, 2nd Ed. Madrid: Visor, 1997.

von Bertalanffy, L. (1968). *General Systems Theory.* New York: Ballantine.

Washburn, S. (1960). Tools and Human Evolution, *Scientific American,* 203(3):63–75.

Weiner, N. (1948). *Cybernetics.* New York: John Wiley.

——— (1954). *The Human Use of Human Beings: Cybernetics and Society,* 2nd ed. Garden City, NY: Doubleday.

Weinrich, J.D. (1980). Toward a sociobiological theory of emotions. In: *Emotions: Theory, Research and Experience,* Vol. 2, ed. R. Plutchik & H. Kellerman. Cambridge, MA: Academic Press.

Werner, H. & Kaplan, B. (1963). *Symbol Formation.* New York: J. Wiley, 1967.

Wertsch, J.V. (1985). *Vygotsky and the Social Formation of Mind.* Cambridge, MA: Harvard University Press.

——— (1991). *Voices of the Mind.* Cambridge, MA: Harvard University Press.

Westrup, J.A., & Harrison, F.W., eds. (1959). *Collins Music Encyclopedia.* Glasgow: William Collins & Sons, Ltd.

White, H. (1980). The Value of Narrativity in the Representation of Reality. In *On Narrative,* ed. W.J.T. Mitchell. Chicago: University of Chicago Press.

Whitehead, A.N. (1927). *Symbolism: It's Meaning and Effect.* New York: Fordham University Press.

Wilson, E.O. (1978). *On Human Nature.* Cambridge, MA: Harvard University Press.

——— (1998). *Consilience.* New York: Vintage Books.

——— (2012). *The Social Conquest of the Earth.* New York: Liveright Publishing Corporation.

Weiner, N. (1950). *The Human Use of Human Beings.* New York: Da Capo Press Science Series.

Wittgenstein, L. (1922). *Tacticus Logico-Philosophicus.* New York: Harcourt, Brace and Co.

Worringer, W. (1908). *Abstraction and Empathy*. Chicago: Elephant Paperbacks, Ivan R. Dee, 1997.

Wurmser, L. (1977). A Defense of the Use of Metaphor in Analytic Theory Formation. *Psychoanalytic Quarterly* 46: 466–498.

Index

re-presentation and, 88, 105, 133,
135, 139–40, 144
See also brain; enteric nervous
system; evolution; genetic code

object constancy
Freud, dreams, and, 24, 123
internal images and, 24, 123
language and, 24
obsessional interference, 99
organic, the
and the cultural, 98, 113, 116
and the symbolic, 83, 85, 93, 113
organic codes, 12, 28, 60, 104
assigning meaning to, 85
Marcello Barbieri and, 103, 104,
116, 118, 141–43
neural codes, cultural codes, and,
97, 98, 103, 116, 117, 141, 143,
148
organic processes, 34
neural processes and, 28, 44, 93, 97,
144–45
organic semiosis, 88, 118
neural semiosis, cultural semiosis,
and, 92
organic transmission, 147–48
organismic model, 66, 82–83, 97
organization, mental/cognitive, 99
oro-facial gestural-mimetic complex, 62
oro-gestural communication, 113, 124,
133. *See also* gestures
oro-gestural origins of language, 61
oro-gestural sign use, 133, 148

Panksepp, J., 103

Panovsky, E., 136
paradigms for change and changing
paradigms, 67–72
pars pro toto, 33, 46. *See also*
synechdoche
parsimony, principle of, 99
phase-transitions, 100, 103, 105, 112
phonologizing gestures, 62
Piaget, Jean, 24–26, 34, 85
pictograms, 135–36
pictographic cognition, 93, 136
pictographic processes, 122, 136, 137,
150, 151
pictographs, 36
pictorial representation, 33, 46
play (speech function), 73
poetic function of speech, 74
preservation, principle of, 99
primary and secondary process
(principles of mental
functioning), 24–25, 28, 33, 45,
48, 52, 61, 62, 64, 81, 93, 111,
122, 123, 147
Interpretation of Dreams and, 28,
32–33, 45, 111, 122, 147
nature of, 25, 28, 45, 57
topographical model and, 20, 24,
28–29, 45, 57
primary process, 38, 49, 124
dreams and, 2, 4, 28–29, 31–33, 35,
36, 38, 43, 45, 55, 93, 111, 122,
123, 129, 137, 139
mechanisms of, 22–23, 33, 36, 38,
46
probability, principle of, 99
"Project for a Scientific Psychology"

(Freud), 14

proprioception, 121, 132, 133

protein coding, 143. *See also* coding

protein synthesis, 88, 118, 143

proto-self, 121

proto-semiotic forms, 46, 59, 60, 66, 69–70

    dreams and, 29, 32, 46, 145

proto-subjectivity, 131–32

psychoanalysis

    background and origin of, 13–16

    nature of, 66

    place in the sciences, 67

    See also specific topics

psychograms, 135–36

psychosis, 25, 62, 63

re-cognition, 37

re-externalization, 96, 146

re-presentation, 9, 38, 81

    coded ideas and, 147, 150, 151

    defined, 38

    dreams and, 5, 23, 38, 52, 82, 88, 122, 123, 133, 136, 137, 145–46

    evolution, epigenesis, and, 6, 82, 88, 92, 96, 104, 122, 129–34, 137, 139, 140

    meaning and, 104, 123, 133–34, 136

    memory and, 70, 132–34

    metaphor and, 88

    neurobiology and, 88, 105, 133, 135, 139–40, 144

    overview and nature of, 5, 38, 112, 144

    regression and, 15, 25

    semiosis and, 6, 23, 69–70, 81, 88, 92, 104, 112, 137, 140, 145–47

    signifying modes and, 139, 150, 151

    tree of, 140

    See also representation; sign representation

ready-made structure (Freud), 123, 138, 145, 147

reference

    acts of, 149

    forms of, 10, 85

    frames of, 97, 98

referenced signifiers, 139

referential distance, 137

referential hierarchy, 115

regression, 71, 82, 83

    dream-thoughts and, 33, 111, 145

    dreams and, 4, 26, 33, 45, 111, 123, 137, 145

    epigenesis and, 71, 99 (*see also* epigenesis)

    forms of, 15, 25, 45

    topographical model and, 25, 28

representation, 139

    epigenesis of, 139

    means of, 22

    reference and, 149

    tree of, 130

    See also re-presentation

repression, 14, 15, 83

    primal organic vs. pathogenic, 15

repression barrier, 14, 16, 24–25

Russell, Bertrand, 60–61, 91, 144, 152

schematization, dynamic, 5, 34, 85

science, 15, 60–61, 67, 68, 84

    aim of, 70

www.ingramcontent.com/pod-product-compliance
Lightning Source LLC
Chambersburg PA
CBHW060221030426
42335CB00015B/1805